The 1997 National Study of the Changing Workforce

By James T. Bond, Ellen Galinsky, and Jennifer E. Swanberg

Families and Work Institute

Some other Families and Work Institute publications:

The Changing Workforce: Highlights of the National Study (1992)

Reframing the Business Case for Addressing Work-Life Initiatives

Moving from Programs to Culture Change: The Next Stage for the Corporate Work-Family Agenda

The Changing Employer-Employee Contract: The Role of Work-Family Issues

An Examination of the Impact of Family-Friendly Policies on the Glass Ceiling

The Family-Friendly Employer: Examples from Europe

The Corporate Guide to National Dependent Care Resource and Referral Services

College and University Reference Guide to Work-Family Programs

Working Fathers: New Strategies for balancing Work and Family

Community Mobilization: Strategies to Support Young Children and Their Families

ISBN 1-888324-09-0

The 1997 National Study of the Changing Workforce

Copyright © 1998, Families and Work Institute, 330 Seventh Avenue, New York, NY 10001. All rights reserved. 212-465-2044. Web site: http://www.familiesandwork.org

The 1997 National Study of the Changing Workforce would not have been possible without the help and financial support of the following co-sponsors:

Lead sponsor: KPMG Peat Marwick LLP

Allstate Insurance Company

The Boeing Company

Ceridian

Citibank, N.A.

The Commonwealth Fund

Fannie Mae

GE Fund

IBM Corporation

Johnson & Johnson

Merck & Co., Inc.

Mobil Corporation

NCR Corporation

Salt River Project

Xerox Corporation

Contributor: WFD

Families and Work Institute

Families and Work Institute is a non-profit organization that addresses the changing nature of work and family life. The Institute is committed to finding research-based strategies that foster mutually supportive connections among workplaces, families, and communities.

Families and Work Institute's
Corporate Leadership Circle

Our thanks to these companies for providing annual donations for general operating support of the Institute.

Corporate Benefactors ($15,000 or more)
AT&T
Johnson & Johnson
Joseph E. Seagram & Sons, Inc.
Merck & Co.

Corporate Patrons ($10,000–$14,999)
Aetna, Inc.
Chase Manhattan Bank, N.A.
Chevron Corporation
Eli Lilly and Company
IBM Corporation
Warner Lambert Corporation
Xerox Corporation

Corporate Sponsors ($5,000–$9,999)
Ceridian Corporation
Corporate Family Solutions
Fel-Pro Incorporated
Marriott International
Price Waterhouse
State Farm Insurance
Texas Instruments
WFD

Corporate Friends ($1,000–$4,999)
Baxter Healthcare Corporation
Chubb Group of Insurance Companies
CIGNA Corporation
Family Education Network
Gannett
GTE
John Hancock Mutual Life Insurance Company
Mutual of New York
Time Warner, Inc.

Acknowledgements

The authors would like to thank the following individuals who have contributed immeasurably to *The 1997 National Study of the Changing Workforce* (NSCW):

- Bernie Milano of KPMG Peat Marwick, the lead sponsor of the 1997 study, for his generous assistance and exceptionally wise counsel;

- Charlie Duckworth, Kathy Haake, Jan Miller, Jerry Shapiro, and Karen L. Smith of Salt River Project, the lead sponsor of the 1992 study, for their vision and commitment to making the idea for this research program a reality;

- Dana E. Friedman, cofounder of Families and Work Institute, for her important role in the 1992 study that led the way;

- all the representatives from our co-sponsoring organizations for serving as true intellectual partners in this study, every step of the way: Bernie Milano, Ned Steele, and Lisa King of KPMG Peat Marwick LLP; Nancy Berry, Sandy Hamilton, and Pam Tvrdy of Allstate Insurance Company; Peter Conte, Kim Frerichs, Carol Larson, Bev Pizzano, and Shannon Russell of the Boeing Company; Norma Anderson, Kathy Fahnhorst, Victor Rutstein, and Linda Hall Whitman of Ceridian; Susan Crown, Judith Fullmer, and Denise Montana of Citibank, N.A.; Michele Yellowitz and Kathryn Taaffe McLearn of The Commonwealth Fund; Kate Fralan, Jodi Fuller, Mary Beth O'Donnell, and Sylvia Padilla of Fannie Mae; Eugene Andrews, Ethan Loney, and Jane Polin of the GE Fund; Ted Childs, Peter Haddad, and Susan Hoeft of the IBM Corporation; Chris Kjeldsen of Johnson & Johnson; Gwen Fisher, Michele Peterson, and Michael Watts of Merck & Co., Inc.; Derrick Hinmon and Allison Wu of the Mobil Corporation; Marilyn Orr and Mindy Tatham of the NCR Corporation; Earline Foster, Kathy Haake, and George Sarkisian of Salt River Project; and Brent Laymon and Marilyn Timbers of the Xerox Corporation;

- Mary Herdoiza and Joyce Moscato of Abernathy/Anderson for understanding the story and for being creative and insightful about media relations;

- WFD, whose contribution helped cover the cost of graphic design;

- Richard P. Shore of Cornell University, who "fathered" this line of research when he was at the U.S. Department of Labor (DOL) and who helped us turn the Quality of Employment Survey (QES), which he had overseen at DOL, into an ongoing research effort of the Families and Work Institute;

- Graham Staines, one of the original researchers involved in the 1977 QES, for his thoughtful assistance in comparing data from the 1977 QES and the 1997 NSCW;

- our colleagues at Louis Harris and Associates for developing the CATI version of the 1997 questionnaire, conducting the telephone interviews, and being an invaluable resource throughout the present study: Humphrey Taylor, David Krane, Amy Cottreau, Paul Rubin, Julie Isbit, and Anne Litke;

- Erik Esckilsen for copyediting the manuscript;

- and, finally, our colleagues at the Families and Work Institute, who have worked creatively and tirelessly on the study from its inception: Amy Rabinowitz for helping secure funding for the research, coordinating with the co-sponsors, and reading and commenting on report drafts; Robin Hardman for directing the communications and publication process and reading and commenting on report drafts; Nik Elevitch for the graphic design and coordination of printing production; John Boose for word processing; Agnieszka Kajrukszto for coordinating endless details and fact-checking; Nina Sazer O'Donnell, Ed Pitt, and Helen Wilkinson for reading and commenting on this report; and Daniel Carlton, Barbara Norcia, and the rest of the FWI staff for all their help with this important study.

Table of Contents

Executive Summary *1*

Chapter 1: Introduction *17*

Chapter 2: Employee Demographics *23*

Chapter 3: Life Off the Job *27*

Chapter 4: Personal Well-Being *57*

Chapter 5: Job Characteristics *69*

Chapter 6: Workplace Characteristics *97*

Chapter 7: Employee Outcomes on the Job *111*

Chapter 8: What Can Employers Do to Improve Satisfaction, Commitment, Performance and Retention? *119*

Chapter 9: Current and Emerging Issues *143*

Technical Appendix *165*

Executive Summary

Synthesis of Findings

The study of work and family life is relatively new. Most studies have investigated either how life on the job affects life at home or, conversely, how life at home affects life on the job. There have been few attempts to connect it all. *The 1997 National Study of the Changing Workforce* provides a model for understanding how work, family, and personal life fit together, a model that incorporates outcomes important to all—productivity and well-being.

We are able to test this model with a nationally representative sample of the U.S. labor force. Our study design also allows us to detect trends through comparisons with the 1977 Quality of Employment Survey, providing a 20-year perspective, and with our 1992 National Study of the Changing Workforce, providing a five-year point of reference.

What have we found?

- The *quality* of workers' jobs and the *supportiveness* of their workplaces are the most powerful predictors of productivity—job satisfaction, commitment to their employers, and retention. Job and workplace characteristics are far more important predictors than pay and benefits, which are generally competitive with the marketplace. To maximize satisfaction, commitment, and retention, employers need to provide high-quality jobs—whatever the employee's occupation—and supportive workplaces—whatever the industry.

  We also found that the characteristics of jobs and workplaces have important effects on the personal lives of workers.

- Employees with more difficult, more demanding jobs and less supportive workplaces experience substantially higher levels of negative spillover from work into their lives off the job—jeopardizing their personal and family well-being.

  These effects set in motion a chain reaction.

- When workers feel burned-out by their jobs, when they have insufficient time and energy for themselves and their families, when work puts them in a bad mood—these feelings spill back into the workplace, limiting job performance.

- Although more supportive workplaces offer some protection against the effects of hectic and demanding jobs, not even the most supportive workplace can eliminate this problem entirely. To improve and sustain productivity over the long run, employers must not only create supportive workplace environments, but also work with employees to keep job demands in check so they do not endanger personal and family well-being. Promoting work-life balance appears to be good both for employees and the bottom line.

So what does the scorecard tell us? Are characteristics of jobs and workplaces improving for the U.S. wage and salaried labor force? There is good news and bad news.

The good news: The quality of jobs has improved somewhat over the past 20 years, and workplaces appear to have become a bit more supportive even over the past five years. There is, however, still plenty of room for improvement.

The bad news: Jobs have become less secure. They have also become more demanding—more time-consuming and more hectic—making it increasingly difficult to achieve a balance between work and personal life.

Meanwhile, what is happening on the home front?

- The proportion of employees living in dual-earner families has increased markedly over the past 20 years, and in three-quarters of these couples, both partners work full-time. Thus, among married employees, the pooled time available for child care (if they have children) and household work is decreasing, creating additional stresses off the job.

In response to this situation, the roles of employed married men and women appear to be converging somewhat.

- Although employed married women still spend more time than men doing household chores, men's time doing household chores has increased over the past 20 years, while women's time has decreased somewhat.

- And although employed married mothers still spend more time than fathers with their children, the time that fathers spend with their children has increased over the past 20 years. The time mothers spend with their children has remained about the same despite an increase in the average hours they spend at their jobs. As a result, children appear to spend somewhat more time with their employed parents today than children 20 years ago did.

Although these role changes with respect to child care and household work appear to be positive, effective responses to the challenges facing today's families, they impose costs as well.

- Employed married men and women have less time for themselves today than their counterparts did 20 years ago, and less time for oneself is associated with lower personal well-being and greater susceptibility to negative spillover from job to home.

This brings us back to work. High-quality jobs—jobs that offer autonomy, learning opportunities, meaning, and a chance to get ahead—energize employees and win their commitment. Supportive workplaces help employees be more effective workers, people, and parents. Employers who can provide these better quality jobs and supportive workplaces have a clear competitive edge.

Summary of the Report

The National Study of the Changing Workforce (NSCW) is a research program of the Families and Work Institute that surveys representative samples of the nation's labor force every five years. This report focuses on findings from the 1997 survey but also provides a historical perspective by comparing data from 1997 with data from the 1992 NSCW and from the U.S. Department of Labor's 1977 Quality of Employment Survey. Only data for wage and salaried workers who are 18 years or older are considered here. The sample sizes are 2,877 employees for 1997, 2,958 for 1992, and 1,298 for 1977.

In recent years, there has been much discussion about the relationship between workers' lives on and off the job, about changes in the nature of work and in the lives of workers, and about the fit between what is good for employers and for employees, including their families. Our study addresses many of the issues raised in this ongoing discussion, while informing it with new insights.

To guide our analyses and frame our presentation of findings, we developed a conceptual model that ties together many of the elements embodied in discussions of work and personal life. This model, outlined below, portrays hypothesized causal pathways connecting characteristics of employees' jobs and workplaces, characteristics of their lives off the job, and aspects of their personal well-being to one another, as well as to the outcomes of primary interest to employers—job satisfaction, commitment to employer, job performance, and retention—at the pinnacle of the pyramid.

> The findings reported here will be of interest not only to employers, but to labor organizations, researchers in various disciplines, public policymakers, and workers everywhere whose experiences and opinions are the substance of the study.

The findings reported here will be of interest not only to employers, but to labor organizations, researchers in various disciplines, public policymakers, and workers everywhere whose experiences and opinions are the substance of the study.

Key findings are summarized below. First, we present descriptive information about the demographic characteristics of individual employees, the characteristics of their lives off the job, their personal well-being, the quality of their jobs, and the quality of their workplaces, as well as their job satisfaction, commitment to their employers, job performance, and plans to remain with their current employers. Then we present and discuss findings that test the conceptual model by exploring the ways in which these factors affect one another.

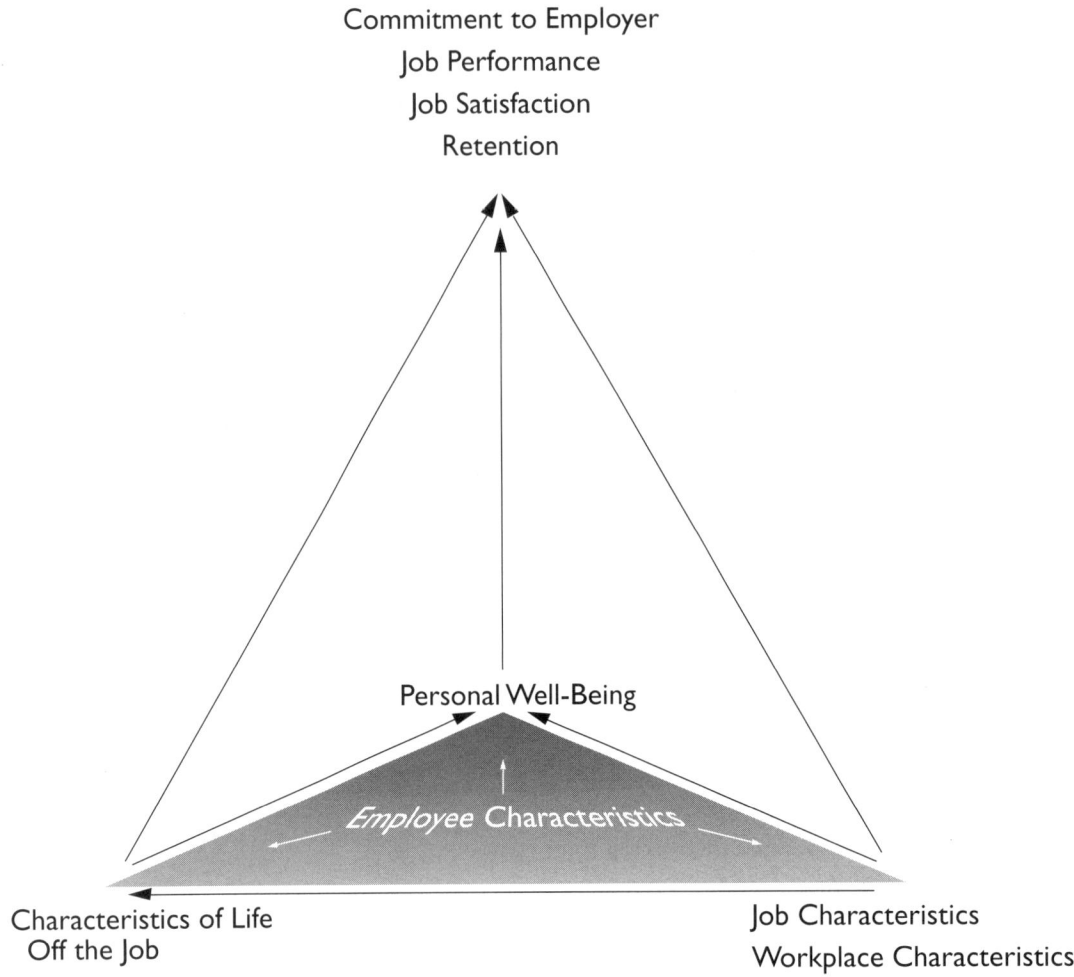

Findings from Chapter 2

The Changing Composition of the Workforce

Over the past 20 years, the U.S. wage and salaried labor force has become more balanced with respect to gender, older on average, much better educated, more racially and ethnically diverse, and more concentrated in managerial and professional occupations.

Findings from Chapter 3

Life Off the Job

Eighty-five percent of U.S. wage and salaried workers live with family members and have immediate, day-to-day family responsibilities off the job. Family members include anyone related by blood, marriage, or adoption, as well as partners to whom employees are not legally married.

Forty-six percent of wage and salaried workers are parents—that is, they have children under 18 who live with them at least half-time.

Nearly one in five employed parents is single, and more workers are raising children alone today than workers did 20 years ago.

Among employed single parents, 27 percent are men.

More than three out of four married employees have spouses or partners who are also employed—an increase from 66 to 78 percent over the past 20 years. Among full-time employees living in dual-earner households, 75 percent have partners who also work full-time.

While only 49 percent of married male employees with children under 18 had employed partners in 1977, 67 percent do today.

Thirteen percent of wage and salaried workers—83 percent of whom have full-time primary jobs—moonlight at secondary jobs, adding an average of 13 hours per week to the hours they work at their primary jobs. The most important reason employees take second jobs is to earn extra money.

> More than three out of four married employees have spouses or partners who are also employed—an increase from 66 to 78 percent over the past 20 years.

Are the Roles of Mothers and Fathers Changing?

Although employed married fathers spend less *time with children* than employed married mothers do on both workdays and days off work, the time fathers spend with their children has increased substantially over the past 20 years, while the time mothers spend has remained the same. For example, fathers spend an average of 2.3 hours per workday caring for and doing things with their children, an increase of 30 minutes per workday since 1977. In contrast, mothers spend nearly one hour more than fathers (3.2 versus 2.3 hours) with their children on workdays, but the total time they spend has not changed significantly from 1977 to 1997.

> Fathers spend an average of 2.3 hours per workday caring for and doing things with their children, an increase of 30 minutes per workday since 1977.

Primarily as the result of changes in fathers' behavior, children are receiving somewhat more attention from their employed parents today than was the case 20 years ago. However, 70 percent of both fathers and mothers feel they do not have enough time with their children.

Employed married mothers spend more *time on chores* than employed married fathers do on both workdays and days off work, whether or not they have children. However, this gap has narrowed quite substantially over the past 20 years, with fathers spending more time, and mothers less, on household work. The decrease for mothers is more than offset by the increase for fathers. Over the past 20 years, mothers' workday time on chores has decreased by 36 minutes per day, while men's time has increased by one hour.

> Although employed married women spend more *time on chores* than employed married men do on both workdays and days off work, whether or not they have children, this gap has narrowed quite substantially over the past 20 years.

Married employees with children—both fathers and mothers—spend less time on their own *personal activities* today than employees 20 years ago did. The decline has been somewhat more pronounced for fathers than for mothers, suggesting, again, a gradual convergence in the way employed fathers and mothers in couples allocate their time off the job. Fathers spend an average of 1.2 hours engaged in their own free-time activities on workdays, 54 minutes less per workday than 20 years ago. Mothers spend even less time engaged in personal activities on workdays (0.9 hours), 42 minutes less per workday than 20 years ago.

The decrease in time that married fathers spend on themselves suggests where they may have found more time for their children and household work, while the decrease in mothers' time on chores and personal time may help to explain how they have managed to preserve time for their children despite longer hours on the job. The implications of reduced personal time for workers' mental health is another matter.

Child Care Arrangements

Among all employed parents with pre-kindergarten children, two-thirds rely on family members—partners and relatives—as the primary source of care for their youngest children, while a third use non-family arrangements. Among employed parents with employed spouses, 55 percent rely on care by parents or other relatives.

> Among employed parents with employed spouses, 55 percent rely on care by parents or other relatives.

Those experiencing the fewest child care breakdowns—having to make other arrangements because their usual care is not available—use center-based or parental child care.

When one member of a dual-earner couple has to care for a sick child or attend to other needs of children when both are supposed to be at their jobs, 83 percent of employed mothers say they are more likely than their partners to take time off, compared with only 22 percent of fathers who make this claim.

Findings from Chapter 4

The Personal Well-Being of Workers

Most employees are fairly satisfied with their lives in general, their family lives, and their relationships with their partners, but many have reservations. Only 33 percent rate general life satisfaction at the highest level, while 31 percent and 51 percent, respectively, rate family satisfaction and marital satisfaction at the highest levels.

In the past three months, nearly one-quarter of employees have felt nervous or stressed often or very often, and 13 percent have had difficulty coping with the demands of everyday life often or very often.

Substantial numbers of employees feel burned-out by their jobs. For instance, in the past three months 26 percent have felt emotionally drained by their work often or very often, and 36 percent have felt used up at the end of the workday often or very often.

Similarly, many employees are affected by negative spillover from their jobs into their personal lives. For example, in the past three months 26 percent have not been in as good a mood as they would have liked at home because of their jobs often or very often, and 28 percent have not had the energy to do things with their families or other important people in their lives often or very often.

> In the past three months nearly one-quarter of employees have felt nervous or stressed often or very often... substantial numbers of employees feel burned-out by their jobs.

Findings from Chapter 5

Job Characteristics

Job Demands

Considering *all paid and unpaid hours worked at any location*, employees spend an average of 44 hours per week on work related to their *primary or only jobs*—six hours more than they are scheduled to work. When the time that the 13 percent of employees who worked at secondary jobs is included, the average total hours worked per week at *all jobs* for all employees increases to 46. On average, men work more hours at all jobs (49 hours per week) than women (42 hours per week).

Eighty-five percent of workers in the wage and salaried labor force are scheduled to work full-time at their main jobs. Women are more likely (21 percent) than men (8 percent) to have part-time jobs, which accounts for part of the difference in hours worked by men and women in the labor force.

It appears[1] that employees are working longer hours today than employees 20 years ago worked. Among employees working 20 or more hours per week,[2] all paid and unpaid hours worked at all jobs have increased from 43.6 hours in 1977 to 47.1 hours in 1997—an increase of 3.5 hours per week. While men's total hours at all jobs have increased from 47.1 hours to 49.9 hours—an increase of 2.8 hours per week—women's hours have increased from 39 hours to 44 hours—an increase of 5 hours per week.

> Among employees working 20 or more hours per week,[1] all paid and unpaid hours worked at all jobs have increased from 43.6 hours in 1977 to 47.1 hours in 1997.

Employed fathers with children under 18 work longer paid and unpaid hours at all jobs (50.9 hours) than other men (48 hours), while employed mothers with children under 18 work fewer hours (41.4 hours) than other women (43.4 hours). Fathers' total work time has increased by 3.1 hours in the past 20 years, while mothers' time has increased by 5 hours.

Given the hours people work, it should come as no surprise that many employees (63 percent) would like to work less. There is no difference in the proportions of men and women who would like to work fewer hours, and both would reduce their current total work week by about 11 hours on average if they could. The proportion of employees who would like to work fewer hours has increased by 17 percentage points since 1992.

---

1. Small variations in the way work hours were measured in 1977 and 1997 may affect these estimates somewhat. However, the differences found are sufficiently large and reliable to suggest that they are not accounted for by measurement bias.

2. The restriction of the sample to employees working 20 or more hours per week was necessitated by the design of the 1977 survey.

Nearly one in five employees is *required* to work paid or unpaid overtime hours once a week or more with little or no notice, and one in five employees regularly takes overnight business trips.

One in three employees brings work home once a week or more often—an increase of 10 percentage points since 1977.

Moreover, many workers indicate that they have to work very fast (68 percent), have to work very hard (88 percent), and do not have enough time to finish everything that needs to get done on the job (60 percent)—much higher proportions than 20 years ago.

> It appears that work has become substantially more demanding over the past 20 years.

To the extent that comparisons with data from 1977 are possible, it appears that work has become substantially more demanding over the past 20 years.

Job Quality

Employees in 1997 have more job autonomy than employees did 20 years ago.

Opportunities and challenges to learn on the job and the meaning that employees find in their work have also increased substantially over this period.

However, only 16 percent of workers rate their chances for advancement in their jobs as excellent, while 23 percent say their chances are good and 61 percent say their chances are fair or poor.

> Only 16 percent of workers rate their chances for advancement in their jobs as excellent... and 61 percent say their chances are fair or poor.

And about three out of 10 employees think it is somewhat or very likely they will lose their jobs in the next couple of years—a higher proportion than 20 years ago.

Compensation and Fringe Benefits

The majority of employees—from 74 through 84 percent—have access to traditional fringe benefits: personal health insurance coverage, pension or retirement plan, paid vacation days and holidays, and paid time off for personal illness. However, only a minority have access to dependent-care benefits: child care information and referral services (20 percent), elder care information and referral services (25 percent), on- or near-site child care services (11 percent), financial assistance for purchasing child care services (13 percent), and dependent-care assistance plans (29 percent).

Historical comparisons could only be made with data from the 1992 survey, and then, only for 5 benefits: personal health insurance coverage, family health insurance coverage, child care information and referral services, employer operated or sponsored on- or near-site child care centers, and elder care information and referral services. Of these fringe benefits, only access to elder care information and referral services has changed, increasing from 11 percent five years ago to 25 percent today.

Access to fringe benefits varies according to a number of factors. Employees who work for companies with larger numbers of employees nationwide have greater access than other workers both to traditional and dependent-care benefits. Part-time workers, low-wage workers, and, to a lesser extent, hourly workers have less access than other workers to traditional fringe benefits.

> Of all dependent care benefits, only access to elder care information and referral services has changed, increasing from 11 percent five years ago to 25 percent today.

Findings from Chapter 6

Workplace Characteristics

Flexible Work Arrangements

Forty-five percent of employees are able to choose—within some range of hours—when they begin and end their workdays, but only one in four can change daily schedules as needed.

Two-thirds (66 percent) of employees find it relatively easy to take time off during the workday to address family or personal matters. However, only 50 percent of employed parents are able to take a few days off from work to care for sick children without losing pay, forfeiting vacation time, or having to fabricate some excuse for missing work.

> Only 50 percent of employed parents are able to take a few days off from work to care for sick children without losing pay, forfeiting vacation time, or having to fabricate some excuse for missing work.

Nearly all employees in companies of all sizes say that women are able to take time off—without jeopardizing their jobs—to recuperate from childbirth, and most say that men can similarly take some time off when they become fathers.

Part-time employees are more likely to believe they could switch to full-time in their current jobs, if they wanted to, than full-time workers are to believe they could switch to part-time in their current positions.

Nineteen percent of employees spend at least part of their *regular workweek* working at home, while another seven percent say they would be allowed to do so if they wanted to.

Work Environment

Most employees feel that their immediate supervisors are quite supportive, with 76 through 92 percent agreeing with nine statements describing various dimensions of supervisor support related to performance of the job and personal or family needs.

Although most employees also feel that the cultures of their workplaces are person- and family-friendly, supervisors are rated more favorably than workplaces. Employees in smaller workplaces rate their workplace cultures as more supportive than employees in larger workplaces do.

And most employees have positive, supportive relationships with coworkers.

Men are slightly more confident than women that employees of their same gender and racial or national backgrounds can advance in the organizations where they work, while non-minority employees are much more confident than minority employees that workers of their own gender and racial or national backgrounds can advance.

Almost one in five employees feels that he or she has been discriminated against at his or her *current* job because of age, gender, or race.

Despite signs of perceived inequality of opportunity and discrimination on the job, 91 percent of workers agree strongly or somewhat that they are treated with respect at work.

> Employees in smaller workplaces rate their workplace cultures as more supportive than employees in larger workplaces do.

Findings from Chapter 7

Employee Outcomes on the Job

Employees are generally satisfied with their jobs—somewhat more so today than employees 20 years ago were, and most are also committed to the success of their companies and loyal to their employers, despite the flagging loyalty of employers to their employees.

More than three out of five employees (62 percent) plan to stay with their current employers for at least the next year, while 22 percent say it is somewhat likely they will make a genuine effort to find another job with another employer in the next year. Only 15 percent indicate that it is very likely they will move on in the next year. Perhaps surprisingly, these proportions have not changed in the past two decades.

> The proportions of employees planning to stay with their employers for at least a year as well as those planning to move on have not changed since 1977.

Executive Summary

Most employees are able to manage their personal lives so that there is relatively little negative spillover from home to work. As an example, only 4 percent of employees reported that their family or personal lives often or very often kept them from getting work done on time at their jobs in the past three months, while 13 percent said this had happened sometimes. The pattern is similar for the other home spillover items. Indeed, reported spillover from home to work is much less frequent than spillover from work to home. Nonetheless, for some employees, spillover from their personal lives into work *is* substantial.

Findings from Chapter 8

What Can Employers Do to Improve Job Satisfaction, Commitment, Performance, and Retention?

Chapters 8 and 9 explore relationships among various parts of the conceptual model that have been described above and discuss the implications of these findings for employers.

Wages and fringe benefits—including traditional benefits like health insurance, pensions, and paid time off, as well as dependent-care benefits like child care information and referral services and on- or near-site centers—are often considered primary determinants of job satisfaction, commitment, loyalty to employer, job performance, and retention.

Findings from the survey, however, tell quite a different story. The quality of employees' jobs and the supportiveness of their workplaces are far more important predictors of these outcomes than earnings or fringe benefits. Job quality is defined as autonomy on the job, learning opportunities, meaningfulness of work, opportunities for advancement, and job security. Workplace support is defined as flexibility in work arrangements, supervisor support, supportive workplace culture, positive coworker relations, absence of discrimination, respect in the workplace, and equal opportunity for workers of all backgrounds.

The implications for employers are potentially far-reaching. While offering competitive pay and benefits is undoubtedly necessary to achieving business goals, it is insufficient on its own. If employers want to maximize satisfaction, commitment, performance, and retention, they must provide high-quality jobs—whatever the employee's occupation—and supportive workplaces—whatever the industry. And improving job quality and work environments is generally much more challenging than providing more pay

> If employers want to maximize satisfaction, commitment, performance, and retention, they must provide high-quality jobs—whatever the employee's occupation—and supportive workplaces—whatever the industry.

or offering new benefits, because it requires organizational change.

Findings related to job performance provide additional insights into how job and workplace characteristics are related to important business outcomes. Job performance is affected by many things, including spillover from problems that employees have in their personal lives. To improve job performance, employers frequently offer special work-life programs—wellness programs, employee assistance programs, child and elder care information and referral services, direct child care services, and so forth—to help employees solve personal problems so they will not spill over into the workplace and reduce productivity. Such strategies generally treat employees' personal problems as products of their lives off the job that are unrelated to their work experiences.

Our findings, however, indicate that work life is actually an important *source* of employees' personal problems. That is, demanding jobs and unsupportive workplaces lead to spillover from jobs into workers' personal lives that can create or exacerbate problems off the job that, in turn, spill over into work and diminish productivity. Thus, helping employees to solve problems in their personal lives by providing special programs of assistance—without also reducing the extent to which jobs contribute to these problems—may severely limit the impact of work-life programs on job performance.

Of particular concern are the negative spillover effects that demanding and hectic jobs can have on the quality of workers' personal lives and well-being. When job demands exceed some individually defined level, it seems that not even the most supportive workplaces can fully protect workers from negative job spillover into their personal lives. This spillover is reflected in high stress, poor coping, bad moods, and insufficient time and energy for people who are personally important, creating "problems" that, in turn, spill over into work and impair job performance. Therefore, actions by employers to not only increase the supportiveness of workplaces, but urge and help employees "get a life" off the job may be crucial to improving employee productivity over the long run—not to mention the obvious benefits to workers and their families.

Findings from Chapter 9

Current and Emerging Issues

Generation X

Members of Generation X (workers 18 through 32 years old in 1997) are much better educated, as well as more racially and ethnically diverse, than young workers 20 years ago were.

Married Gen Xers—with and without children—are more likely to have an employed spouse than young workers in 1977 were, and both members of employed couples are more likely to work full-time. This creates stresses and strains that were less prevalent among earlier generations of workers.

Contrary to the portrayal of Generation X in popular media, young workers today are not a group of "slackers." They work substantially longer hours on average and find their jobs more demanding than young workers 20 years ago did.

> Contrary to the portrayal of Generation X in popular media, young workers today are not a group of "slackers."

Although members of Generation X feel somewhat more satisfied with their jobs than young workers did two decades ago, they feel that they have less job security.

Generation-X employees are less likely than Baby Boomers were to have embarked upon their work lives imagining they would remain with the same company for most of their careers. However, half of all Gen Xers *and* Boomers now view expectations of a lifetime job as passé.

Though most Gen Xers do not expect to stay in the same jobs forever, they are not a generation of job-hoppers. Indeed, only 22 percent of young workers in both 1977 and 1997 said it was very likely they would leave their employers within the next year. Moreover, Gen Xers are just as loyal to their employers, and say that they are just as willing to work harder than required for the success of their companies, as older workers.

As for employers' concerns about retaining Gen-X employees, who are in short supply, the findings indicate that higher job quality and workplace support that is responsive to basic individual needs both on and off the job are the factors most likely to increase retention— assuming that wages and fringe benefits are competitive. This is exactly what we found for workers in general.

Elder Care

Historically, and still today, families provide the major part of non-medical care for elderly relatives. As the population ages and labor-force participation expands, however, the supply of non-employed family members available to provide care is not keeping pace with needs. Looking into the future, one sees that elder care will demand time and attention from growing numbers of employees, affecting the way they work.

While only 13 percent of workers were providing special assistance to someone 65 years or older when interviewed, 25 percent—a quarter of the U.S. wage and salaried labor force—had provided elder care during the preceding year.

> 25 percent of employees—a quarter of the U.S. wage and salaried labor force—have provided elder care during the preceding year.

One in five working parents has been part of the so-called "sandwich generation" during the past year—both raising children and caring for elderly relatives.

The proportions of employed men and women with elder care responsibilities are virtually the same.

Employees with elder care responsibilities spend an average of nearly 11 hours per week providing assistance, with men and women spending equal amounts of time.

Among workers who had elder care responsibilities in the past year, more than one-third reduced their work hours or took time off to provide that care. Surprisingly, in the past year employed men with elder care responsibilities were just as likely as employed women to have taken time off or reduced their work hours to provide care.

Many employers appear to be at least informally supportive of workers who need to take time off or reduce work hours to provide elder care. However, employees in managerial and professional positions and employees with higher earnings are more able to take as much time as they need without losing pay.

Only one in four employees has access to elder care resource and referral services through his or her employer.

With today's smaller families, single-parent families, and two-career couples, the pool of able-bodied, non-employed adults available to provide elder care is shrinking just as demand for care is rising. It is not clear that anyone—employees, employers, community agencies, or government—is prepared for the substantial impact that growing elder care responsibilities will have on the labor force in coming years. Although no one expects

> It is not clear that anyone—employees, employers, community agencies, or government—is prepared for the substantial impact that growing elder care responsibilities will have on the labor force in coming years.

employers to address the full range of issues raised by this demographic tidal wave, employers who do not anticipate the potential disruptions to their workforces will likely be taken aback by the consequences.

Work-Family Backlash?

Despite claims in the press and worries in the boardroom, the findings do not indicate that young, unmarried, or childless employees are more likely than other workers to resent work-family benefits that do not benefit them personally. Nor are they more likely to resent doing extra work occasionally to accommodate coworkers' family or personal needs.

In general, the demographic characteristics of individual workers bear little relationship to either their acceptance of work-family benefits that are not personally beneficial to them or their willingness to do extra work to accommodate the personal and family needs of coworkers. Rather, workplace characteristics—flexibility, supportive supervisors, good coworker relations, and supportive workplace cultures—are most predictive of employees' acceptance of work-family benefits and willingness to accommodate coworkers' needs. Thus, it would appear that employers who have made greater progress in creating person- and family-friendly work environments actually experience less work-family backlash.

> Although creating a highly supportive workplace environment is more challenging than simply implementing another discrete benefit or program from the top down, the challenge appears to be well worth the effort.

To a large extent, supportive workplace factors are within the control of employers to alter, unlike the personal demographic characteristics that workers bring to the job. Although creating a highly supportive workplace environment is more challenging than simply implementing another discrete benefit or program from the top down, the challenge appears to be well worth the effort when measured by employees' attitudes and behavior on the job, ranging from less resentment of work-family benefits and greater support of coworkers to increased job satisfaction, commitment, performance, and retention.

1 Introduction

Beginning in 1969, the Department of Labor funded three national studies of the United States workforce as part of the Quality of Employment Survey (QES). The last survey in this series, which was conducted in 1977, marked the first time that research on a large, representative sample of U.S. workers collected information about not only the work lives of employees, but their personal lives as well.[3] When the QES program was halted for a variety of reasons in 1977, a 15-year gap ensued during which there were small scale studies of life on and off the job, but no large-scale nationally representative studies were undertaken.

The Families and Work Institute stepped into this breach in the early 1990s by obtaining private support for the National Study of the Changing Workforce (NSCW) as an ongoing research program of the Institute. The Institute's program is more explicit and comprehensive than the QES in addressing issues related to both work and personal life. It also reflects a strong business perspective, in addition to the broader social and economic perspectives that shaped the QES.

The NSCW surveys representative samples of the nation's labor force every five years, with findings on important and timely issues released during the intervening years through Institute reports, publication in academic journals and books, media coverage, and presentations to audiences of private- and public-sector decision-makers. The first NSCW survey was conducted in 1992;[4] the second, in 1997; and the third is scheduled for 2002. The 1997 survey, the focus of this report, provides a unique opportunity to examine workforce issues through the lens of history with 20-year comparisons to the 1977 QES.

In designing the 1997 study, we have been guided by our exemplary group of co-sponsors, who also fund the research program: KPMG Peat Marwick LLP (lead sponsor); Allstate Insurance Company; The Boeing Company; Ceridian; Citibank, NA; The Commonwealth Fund; Fannie Mae; GE Fund; IBM Corporation; Johnson & Johnson; Merck & Co., Inc.; Mobil Corporation; NCR Corporation; Salt River Project; and Xerox Corporation. The co-sponsors helped us to identify the questions of greatest importance to business and interpret findings from a business perspective. We, of course, assume full responsibility for the final content of this report.

---

3. Quinn, R.P., and Staines, G.L. (1979). *The 1977 Quality of Employment Survey*. Ann Arbor, MI: Institute for Social Research, University of Michigan.

4. Galinsky, E., Bond, J.T., and Friedman, D.E. (1993). *The Changing Workforce: Highlights of the National Study*. New York: Families and Work Institute.

Conceptual Model to Guide Research

What can be done to recruit good employees, maximize their productivity, and retain them within the organization? This question is of continuing and growing concern to employers. While business management has historically focused on issues of wages, fringe benefits, and labor relations to achieve these goals, it is beginning to view more fundamental characteristics of jobs and workplace environments as playing important roles in recruitment, productivity, and retention. Moreover, management has gradually come to understand that employees' lives off the job must be reconciled with their lives on the job if solutions that work for employers, employees, and our society at large are to be found. The widespread development of work-family and work-life initiatives over the past decade is testimony to this change in thinking.

Much historical research treats work life and personal life as separate domains that can be understood independently of one another, while more contemporary research often focuses only on the conflict and interference between work and personal life. To guide our work, we have developed a more inclusive conceptual model, a model that we hope will be useful to decision makers and also move thinking and practice forward. The model is shown on the next page.

At the top of the pyramid are outcomes of particular concern to employers: employee commitment, job performance, and retention. Our study ultimately asks the question: Under what conditions are employees more likely to be committed to their employers, to perform better, and to want to stay with their employers?

At the bottom right point of the pyramid are job and workplace characteristics—earnings and fringe benefits, job demands, job quality, and supportiveness of the workplace environment—all of which can be influenced by the actions of employers and all of which, we hypothesize, might affect employee outcomes, personal well-being, and characteristics of life off the job, as indicated by the arrows pointing in the directions of those points.

> Our study ultimately asks the question: Under what conditions are employees more likely to be committed, to perform better, and to want to stay with their employers?

At the bottom left point of the pyramid are characteristics of employees' personal and family lives off the job, none of which is directly affected by the actions of employers but some of which, we hypothesize, might be affected by job and workplace characteristics as indicated by the direction of the arrow connecting those points. We also hypothesize that off-the-job factors themselves might affect both personal well-being and employee outcomes on the job, as indicated by arrows pointing in those directions.

At the bottom back point is personal well-being, as measured by such factors as life and marital satisfaction, stress and coping, and psychological states related to employment including mood, energy, and job burnout. We hypothesize that personal well-being is affected by characteristics of life off the job and job/workplace characteristics and that it affects employee outcomes on the job as indicated by the upward pointing arrow.

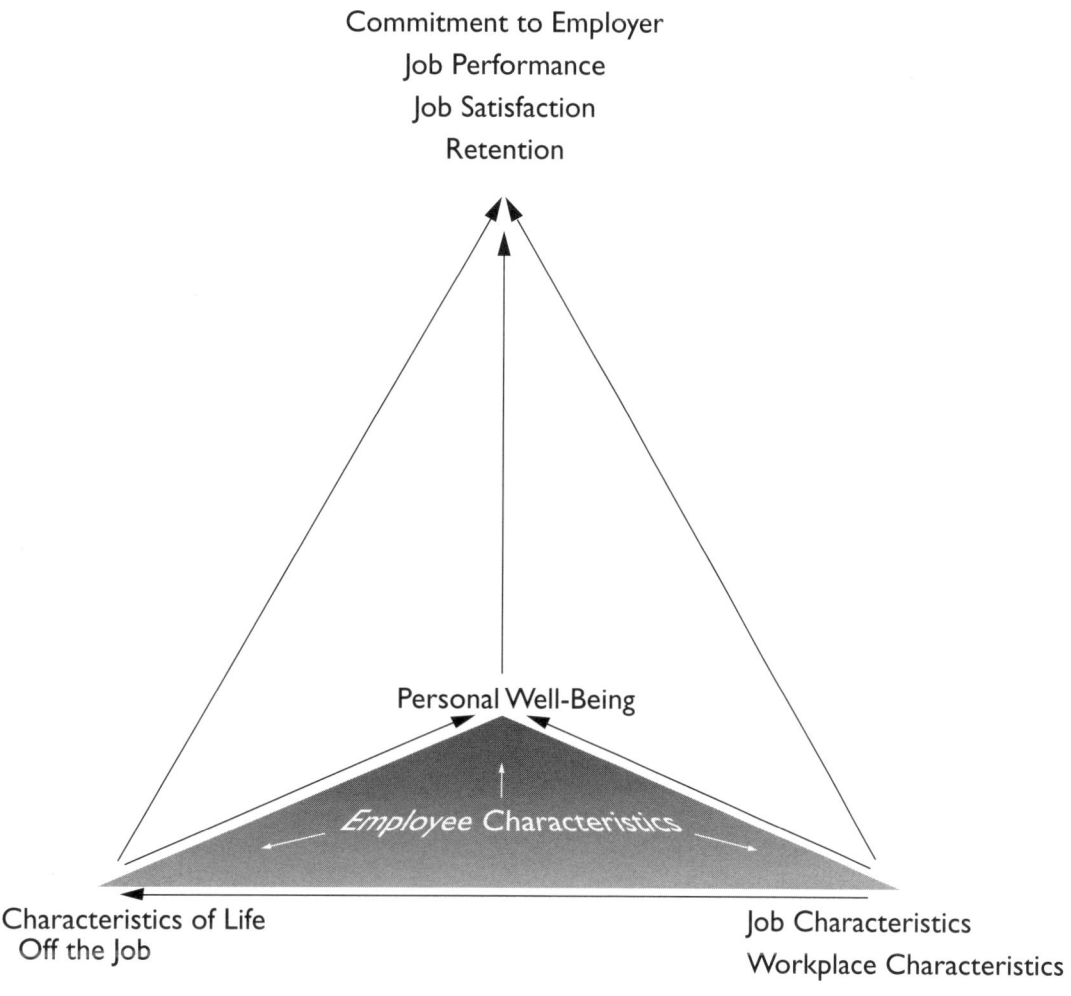

Employee demographics constitute the base of the pyramid: age, gender, race/ethnicity, education, occupation, and years in the labor force. These basic demographic factors are controlled in all multivariate analyses predicting employee outcomes on the job.

The conceptual model implies causality, and later in this report (Chapters 8 and 9), we evaluate some of the causal pathways in the model. Even though cross-sectional survey data does not permit firm conclusions about what causes what, we believe that careful analysis—guided by an explicit conceptual model and tempered by common sense—can be useful in identifying probable causes and their likely relative importance.

We are quick to acknowledge that the conceptual model proposed here is an oversimplification of reality. As we point out in Chapter 8, common sense strongly suggests that within the major causal flows hypothesized in the model, effects may sometimes run in the opposite direction for particular variables. For example, employees who bring work home from the office more frequently—a characteristic of demanding jobs—are also more willing to work harder than they have to in order to help their company succeed—a measure of commitment to the employer. But does bringing work home more often actually cause employees to become more committed to their company's success or does greater commitment cause employees to bring work home more often? Common sense suggests the latter. Although such inconsistencies point the way toward model refinements, we believe that the conceptual model in its simplified form is a good starting point and general guide to making practical sense of our data for employers who must make strategic business decisions on a daily basis, whether or not good information is available.

Study Design, Methodology, and Presentation

Although the 1997 National Study of the Changing Workforce (NSCW) builds upon the 1992 survey, we both added new topics of emerging interest and incorporated, in their precise wording, many of the same questions asked in the 1977 Quality of Employment Survey (QES). Comparisons between the 1997 NSCW and 1977 QES will appear throughout the report to measure changes in the workforce and workplace over the past two decades. Select comparisons of 1997 and 1992 data are also included when most appropriate.

Sampling designs, responses rates, and analytic methods are described in more detail in the Technical Appendix at the end of this report. However, some basic facts are provided here to guide the reader:

- All of the findings presented in this report are based on analyses of data for wage and salaried employees only, although all three surveys also interviewed self-employed workers. The total number of wage and salaried workers interviewed was 2,788 in 1997, 2,958 in 1992, and 1,311 in 1977.

- When comparing data from the 1977 QES and 1997 NSCW, we restricted each sample to reflect the selection criteria of the other. Since the QES surveyed only persons working 20 or more hours per week and only conducted interviews in English, we excluded from the 1997 sample employees working fewer than 20 hours per week or not interviewed in

English. Since the NSCW survey only interviewed persons 18 years and older, we excluded employees younger than 18 from the 1977 QES sample. Therefore when comparing 1997 with 1977 data, the 1997 sample is reduced to 2,725 and the 1977 sample to 1,298.

- When comparing 1992 and 1997 NSCW data, the 1997 sample is reduced to wage and salaried workers under 65 years old to match the 1992 sample. Thus, in 1992 vs. 1997 comparisons, the 1997 sample is 2,773, rather than 2,877.

- In some analyses the reported sample size will be smaller than the total sample either because of missing data or because the question was not asked of respondents who did not meet particular conditions—such as being married or having children.

- Because of rounding errors, when findings are presented as percentage distributions across several responses categories, they do not always add up to 100 percent. With few exceptions, fractional percentages are not reported in order to simplify presentation.

- Whenever we talk about *differences, changes,* and *relationships*, they are statistically significant, unless otherwise noted. The minimum threshold for statistical significance in this report is $p < .01$, meaning that a difference reported as significant would only occur 1 time in 100 by chance. Conversely, 99 times out of 100, such a finding reflects a real difference. Often the differences reported here are much less likely to have occurred by chance: 1 in 1,000; 1 in 10,000; or less likely.

- Marital status and parental status have specific definitions in this report that may vary from the definitions used in other research. We classify employees as married both when they are legally married and when they are living in a relationship with a partner—a relationship that may or may not have legal status under common law depending on the state of residence. Employees are classified as parents when they have dependent children who reside with them and under their custody or guardianship on a half-time basis or more.

2 Employee Demographics

For the purposes of this report, *employee demographics* include only those demographic characteristics that typically become a matter of record upon hiring—gender, age, education, race/ethnicity, work history (specifically, years in the labor force), and occupation. These characteristics form the base of the pyramid representing our conceptual model. Other demographic factors—marital status, parental status, household income, and so forth—are treated as characteristics of life off the job, which are not necessarily known to employers when they hire employees or afterward.

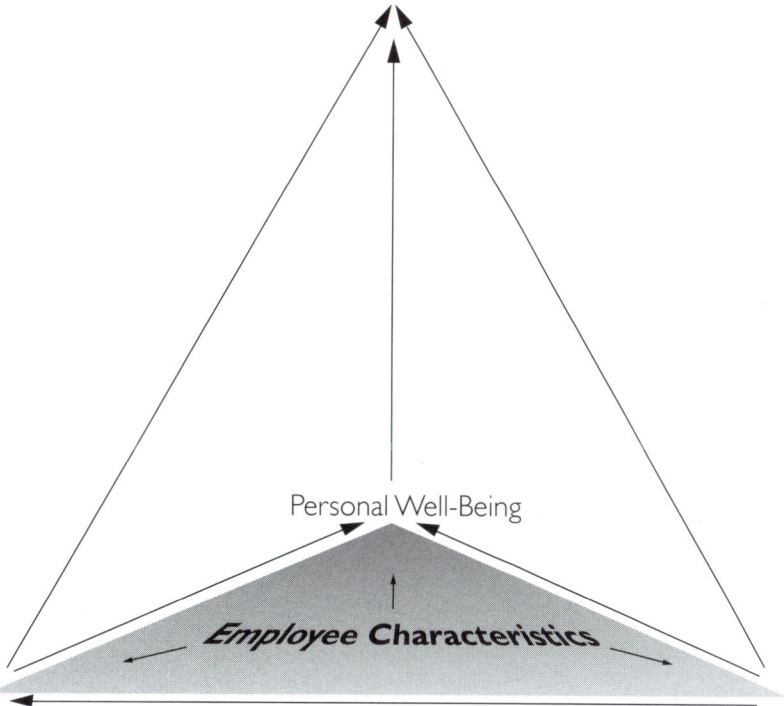

The findings presented in Table 2.1 (Column A) describe the U.S. wage and salaried labor force in 1997. By themselves, these descriptive data offer a point of reference, but without actual comparison to another point—e.g., employees in a particular company, employees in another country, or U.S. employees at another point in time—they mean very little.

To place our 1997 findings in context, we compared them with data from the 1977 Quality of Employment Survey (QES), which is described in the introduction and will be used as a point of comparison throughout this report.[5]

From 1977 to 1997, the U.S. wage and salaried labor force has become more balanced with respect to gender, older on average, much better educated, more racially and ethnically diverse, and more concentrated in managerial and professional occupations.

Our findings are entirely compatible with findings about trends in the U.S. labor force reported by other sources—trends that promise to continue unabated.

---

5. For purposes of comparison, the 1997 sample was reduced to employees working 20 or more hours per week and interviewed in English, while the 1977 sample was reduced to employees 18 and older. Percentages for the 1997 full and reduced samples may differ slightly.

Table 2.1: Demographics for All U.S. Wage and Salaried Employees in 1997 And for Employees Working More Than 20 Hours Per Week in 1997 and 1977

	Column A	**Column B**		
Demographics	Full 1997 Sample	1997 vs. 1977 Restricted Samples for Comparisons[a]		
		NSCW 1997		QES 1977
	Percentage *(sample size)*	Percentage *(sample size)*	Sig.	Percentage *(sample size)*
Gender:	*(n=2877)*	*(n=2725)*	*	*(n=1298)*
Male	52%	53%		58%
Female	48	47		42
Age:	*(n=2839)*	*(n=2688)*		*(n=1280)*
Mean Age in Years	39.7 yrs	39.9 yrs	***	37.3 yrs
Percent distribution by age groups:				
Under 33: Generation-X in 1997	32%	31%	***	46%
33–51: Baby Boom generation	53	54	***	35
over 51: War/Pre-war generations	15	15	ns	19
Education:	*(n=2873)*	*(n=2721)*		*(n=1277)*
High school, GED, or less	36%	36%	***	60%
Some post-secondary education	34	33	**	22
Four-year college degree or more	31	31	***	18
Race or ethnicity:	*(n=2850)*	*(n=2699)*		*(n=1277)*
White	80%	80%	***	88%
African American, black	11	12	ns	9
Other	9	9	ns	3
Work History:	*(n=2838)*	No Comparison Possible		
Years in labor force	19.5 yrs			
Occupation:	*(n=2853)*	*(n=2704)*	***	*(n=1298)*
Managers and professionals	34%	34%		27%
Other occupations	66	66		73

[a] For purposes of comparison, the 1997 NSCW sample was restricted to employees who worked 20 or more hours per week and were interviewed in English, while the 1977 QES sample was restricted to employees 18 or more years old.

Significance: * = $p < .01$; ** = $p < .001$; *** = $p < .0001$.

3 Life Off the Job

The National Study of the Changing Workforce paints a broad and integrated picture of the U.S. labor force—one that encompasses the lives of workers both on and off the job, and relates these two domains. The study is grounded in our belief that a holistic view of workers as people is necessary for developing effective business policy, social policy, and individual solutions. This chapter provides insights into employees' personal lives that are seldom provided by large-scale labor-force research; later chapters explore the relationships between employees' lives off and on the job. Characteristics of life off the job are major elements in our conceptual model.

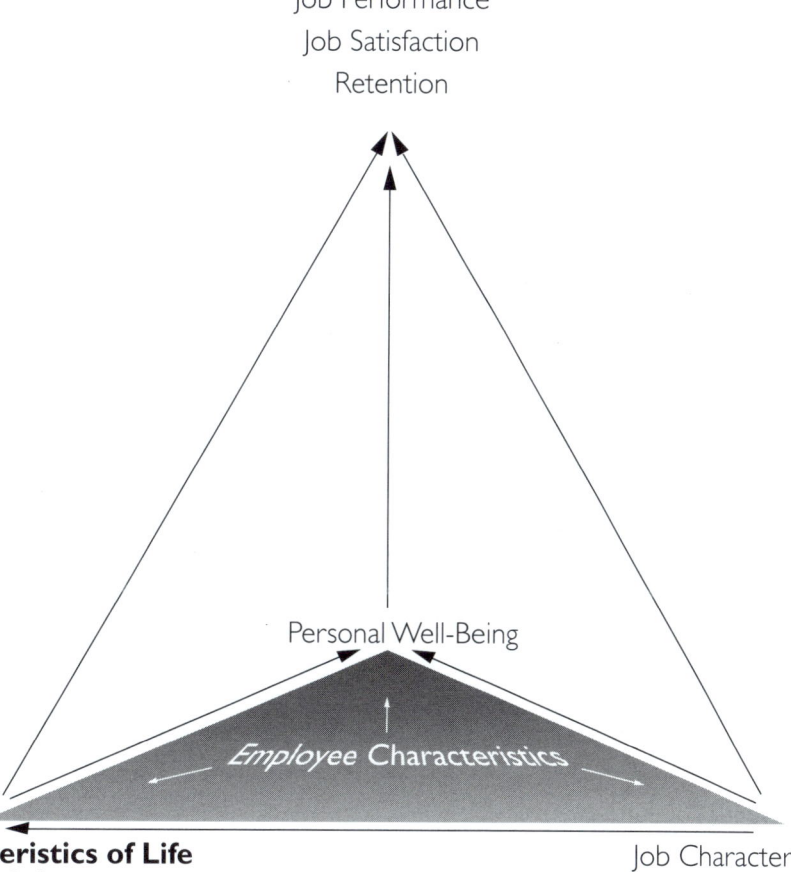

Family/Household Demographics

Four out of five U.S. wage and salaried workers live with family members and, therefore, have immediate, day-to-day family responsibilities off the job.

- Fully 85 percent of employees live in households with family members—defined as persons to whom they are related by marriage, blood, or adoption, as well as partners to whom they are not legally married. Among the 15 percent of workers not living with family members, all have individual and social responsibilities in their personal lives off the job.

Figure 3.1: Living With Family Members

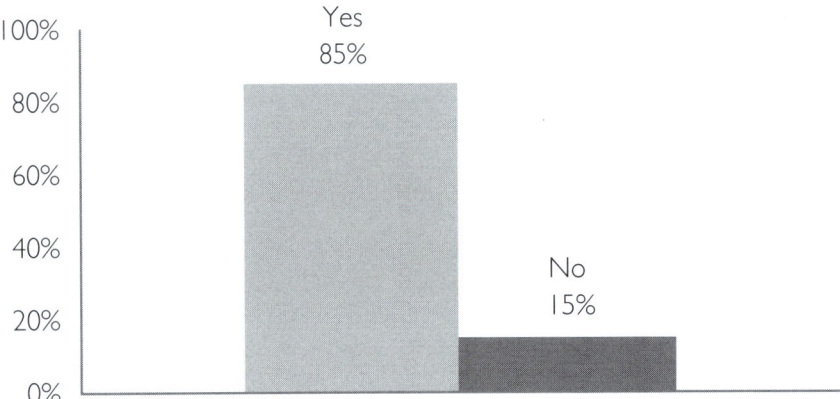

Employees in 1997 are less likely to be legally married than employees in 1977 were, but just as likely to be living in marriage-like relationships.

- Currently, 58 percent of employees are married, and another seven percent report that they live with a partner as a couple. Thus, 65 percent live in marriage-like relationships with either a spouse or partner.

- Although we find that today's employees are less likely to be legally married than employees in 1977 were, employees in 1997 are just as likely as those in 1977 were to live in marriage-like relationships—66 percent overall.[6]

---

6. For purposes of comparison, the 1997 sample was reduced to employees working 20 or more hours per week and interviewed in English, while the 1977 sample was reduced to employees 18 and older. Percentages for the 1997 full and reduced samples may differ slightly.

28 *Life Off the Job*

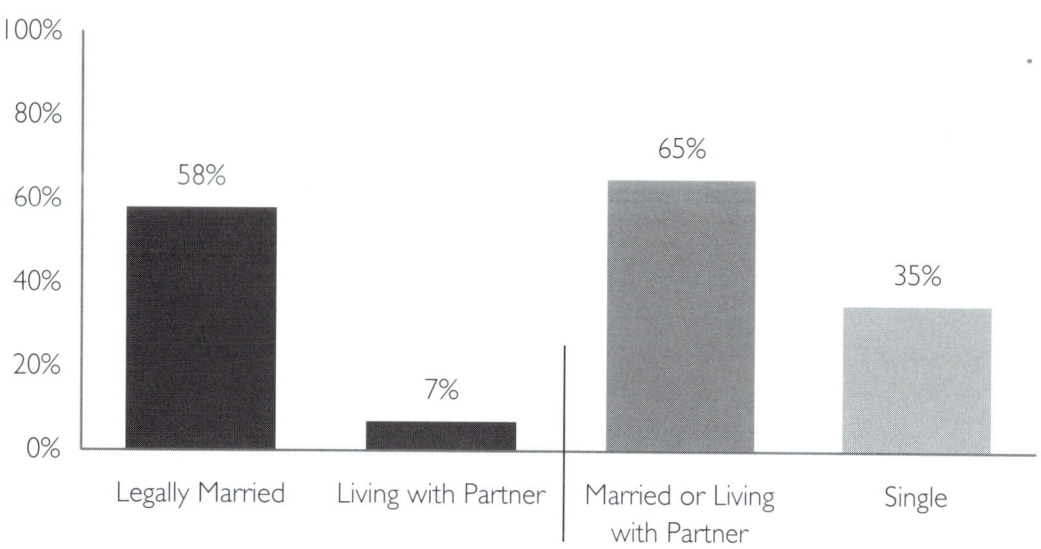

Figure 3.2: Marital Status in 1997

> More than a third of employees in the U.S. workforce have children under 13 requiring care and supervision during work hours, and 46 percent have children under 18 years old at home.

- Almost half of all wage and salaried workers have children under 18 living at home at least half-time. Thirty five percent of workers have children under 13, and almost one in five workers (19 percent) has children under six living at home.

> More than a third of employees in the U.S. workforce have children under 13 requiring care and supervision during work hours, and 46 percent have children under 18 years old at home.

Life Off the Job

Figure 3.3: Parental Status in 1997

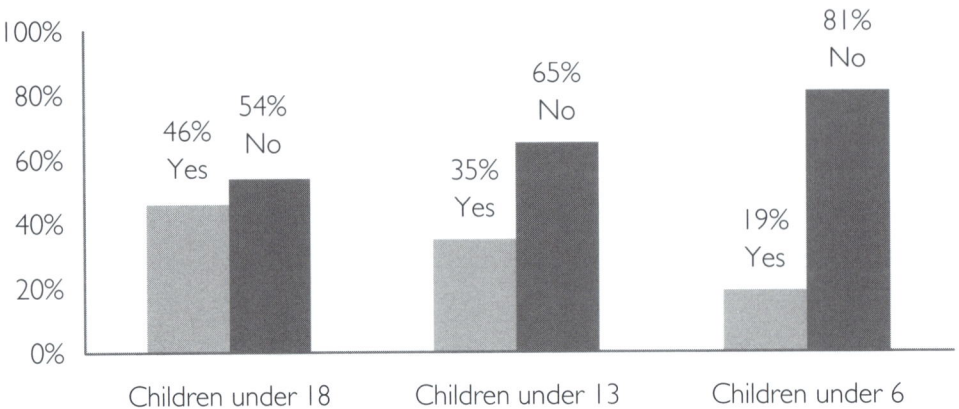

Nearly one in five employed parents is single, and among employed single parents, one out of four is a man. More workers are raising children alone today than 20 years ago.

- Almost 20 percent of employed parents are single and raising their children alone.[7] It is not surprising that single parents are much more likely to be women than men. What is surprising, however, is the substantial number of fathers raising children alone. Among single parents, 27 percent are men. (Figure 3.4)

---

7. Single parent status is defined as not legally married or living in a relationship with a partner, and as having custody of children on a half-time basis or more.

Figure 3.4: Working Parents in 1997

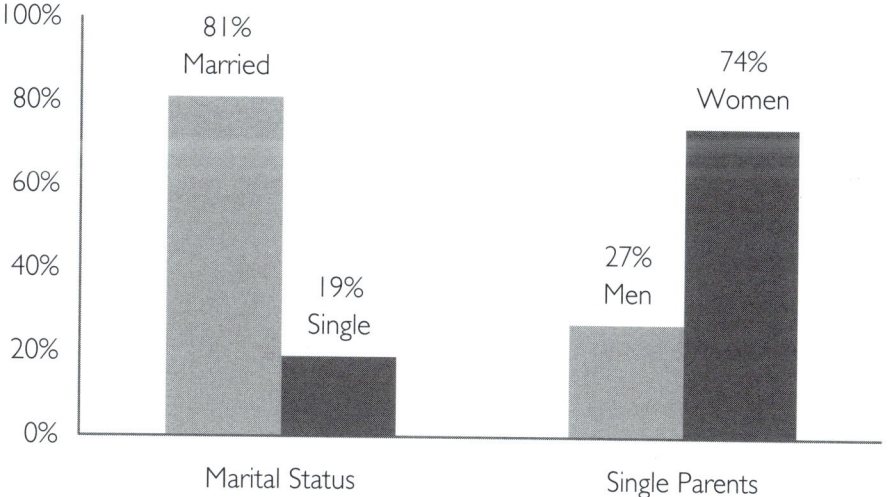

- Comparing parents in 1997 and 1977, we find that today's parents are somewhat more likely to be raising children alone (19 percent) than parents in 1977 (13 percent) were.[8]

Family earnings are somewhat higher for employees with children than for employees without children, but total household income from all sources is the same.

- General findings about family earnings and total household income are presented in Table 3.1. Comparisons of employees with and without children under 18 reveal that employees with children under 18 at home have significantly higher average total family earnings ($60,093) than employees without children ($48,512). In all likelihood, this difference reflects the fact that employed parents are in their prime earning years. No difference was found for total household income from all sources, which was $58,552 for all employees.

Total household income for all employees and for employees with children has not changed significantly from 1977 to 1997.

- Household income has not changed significantly from 1977 to 1997.[3] Expressed in 1997 dollars, it was $55,153 for all workers and $57,594 for workers with children over this 20-year period.

---

8. For purposes of comparison, the 1997 sample was reduced to employees working 20 or more hours per week and interviewed in English, while the 1977 sample was reduced to employees 18 and older. Percentages for the 1997 full and reduced samples may differ slightly.

31 *Life Off the Job*

Table 3.1: Earnings and Income

Income	Mean or Median (sample size)
*Projected 1997 Family **Earnings**:*[a]	
All Employees:	(n=2480)
Mean projected family earnings for 1997	$53,912
Median projected family earnings for 1997	$45,000
Employees with Children Under 18:	(n=1156)
Mean projected family earnings for 1997	$60,093
Median Projected Family Earnings for 1997	$50,000
Employees without Children:	(n=1324)
Mean projected family earnings for 1997	$48,512
Median projected family earnings for 1997	$38,000
*Total Household **Income** from All Sources:*[b]	
All Employees:	(n=2698)
Mean household income from all sources	$58,552
Median household income from all sources	$46,035
Employees with Children Under 18:	(n=1251)
Mean household income from all sources	$59,905
Median household income from all sources	$49,104
Employees without Children:	(n=1447)
Mean household income from all sources	$57,381
Median household income from all sources	$43,989

[a] *Projected family earnings includes only respondents' earnings for single workers. For married/partnered workers, it includes respondent earnings plus any earnings contributed by spouse/partner.*

[b] *Income reported for the 1996 tax year is stated in 1997 dollars.*

Among married employees, men still contribute more to family income than women. The gap narrows among married employees in dual-earner couples.

- Among all married wage and salaried workers, men contribute 75 percent of couples' earnings on average, while women contribute 48 percent—a difference of 27 percentage points (Table 3.2). Note that these percentages do not add up to 100 percent because they do not represent the contributions of partners within the same couple but, instead, the independent contributions to family income of employed married men and women in the labor force. The larger average contribution of men can be explained partly by the fact that men are more likely than women to have full-time jobs, as well as partners who work only part-time or do not work for pay (Figure 3.7).

- Among employees living in dual-earner couples, this disparity narrows only slightly in absolute terms to 23 percentage points. Men contribute 63 percent and women 40 percent to couples' earnings. Men are more likely to have full-time jobs and partners who work part-time.

- The gap narrows even further when we look at dual-earner couples in which both work full-time. In these families, men contribute 59 percent and women 42 percent of couples' earnings—a difference of only 17 percentage points.

- Among employees in dual-earner couples with children under 18, the gap is 25 percentage points, with men contributing 64 percent of couples' earning and women 39 percent.

> In dual-earner families where both partners work full-time, men contribute 59 percent on average, and women 42 percent of couples' earnings—a difference of only 17 percentage points.

Table 3.2: Contributions to Family Income [a]

Income	Percentage (sample size)
Among all *married* wage and salaried workers:	(n=1613)
Men's contribution to couples' earnings	75%
Women's contribution to couples' earnings	48
Among workers in *dual-earner couples*:	(n=1208)
Men's contribution to couples' earnings	63%
Women's contribution to couples' earnings	40
Among workers in *dual-earner couples* in which *both work full-time*:	(n=932)
Men's contribution to couples' earnings	59%
Women's contribution to couples' earnings	42
Among workers in *dual-earner couples with children* under 18:	(n=713)
Men's contribution to couples' earnings	64%
Women's contribution to couples' earnings	39

[a] *These percentages do not add up to 100 percent because they do not represent the contributions of partners within the same couple but, instead, the independent contributions to family income of employed married men and women in the labor force.*

Work-Related Aspects of Life Off of the Job

Significant numbers of wage and salaried workers are moonlighting outside their main jobs, mainly to earn extra money.

- Thirteen percent of wage and salaried employees work at a job in addition to their main job (Figure 3.5).

- By and large, these are not people piecing together part-time jobs to achieve full-time work. More than four in five employees (83 percent) who work more than one job do so in addition to full-time jobs. Whether working full- or part-time at their main jobs, employees working more than one job average about 13.2 hours a week at their other job(s).

> More than four in five employees who work more than one job do so in addition to full-time jobs.

Figure 3.5: Working More Than One Job

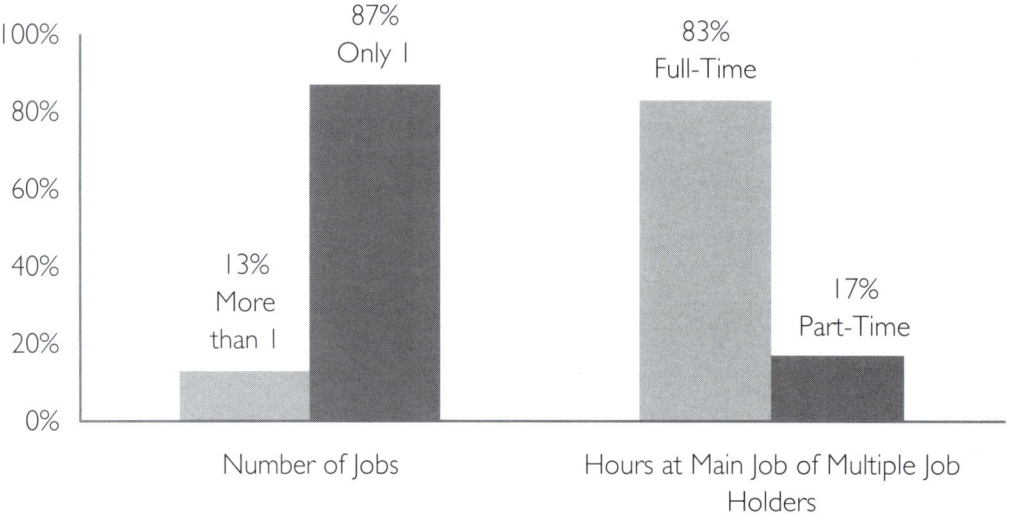

- Why do people moonlight? Almost three quarters (74 percent) of employees working more than one job do so to earn additional income (Figure 3.6). The remaining 25 percent take or create another job or jobs to pursue a favorite hobby (11 percent), to explore alternative career or job options (5 percent), or to secure income in the event that they lose their main jobs (3 percent), or for some other reason (7 percent).

34 Life Off the Job

Figure 3.6: Reasons for Moonlighting

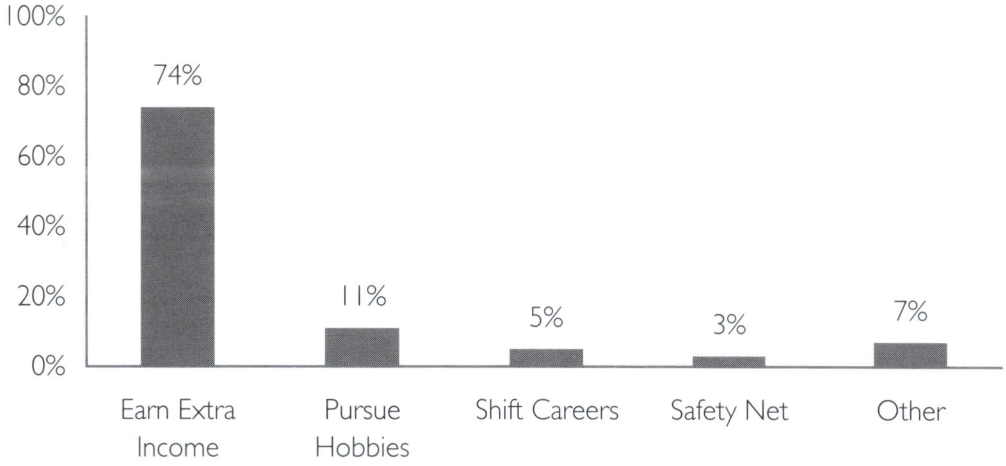

- Earn Extra Income: 74%
- Pursue Hobbies: 11%
- Shift Careers: 5%
- Safety Net: 3%
- Other: 7%

More than three out of four married employees have spouses or partners who are employed—a significant increase over the past 20 years.

- As shown in Figure 3.7, 78 percent of married employees in 1997 live in dual-earner households. Women are still more likely to live with an employed partner (89 percent) than men (69 percent).

- The proportion of married employees living in dual-earner households has increased rapidly over the past 20 years—from 66 percent in 1977 to today's 78 percent.[9]

- Among married employees with children under 18, the proportion who live in dual-earner couples parallels the trend for married couples in general, increasing from 64 percent in 1977 to 78 percent in 1997.

- Among married male employees with children under 18, 49 percent had employed partners in 1977, while 67 percent do today.

> The proportion of married employees living in dual-earner households has increased rapidly over the past 20 years—from 66 percent in 1977 to today's 78 percent.

---

9. For purposes of comparison, the 1997 sample was reduced to employees working 20 or more hours per week and interviewed in English, while the 1977 sample was reduced to employees 18 and older. Percentages for the 1997 full and reduced samples may differ slightly.

Life Off the Job

Figure 3.7: Employment Status of Partners in Married Couple Families

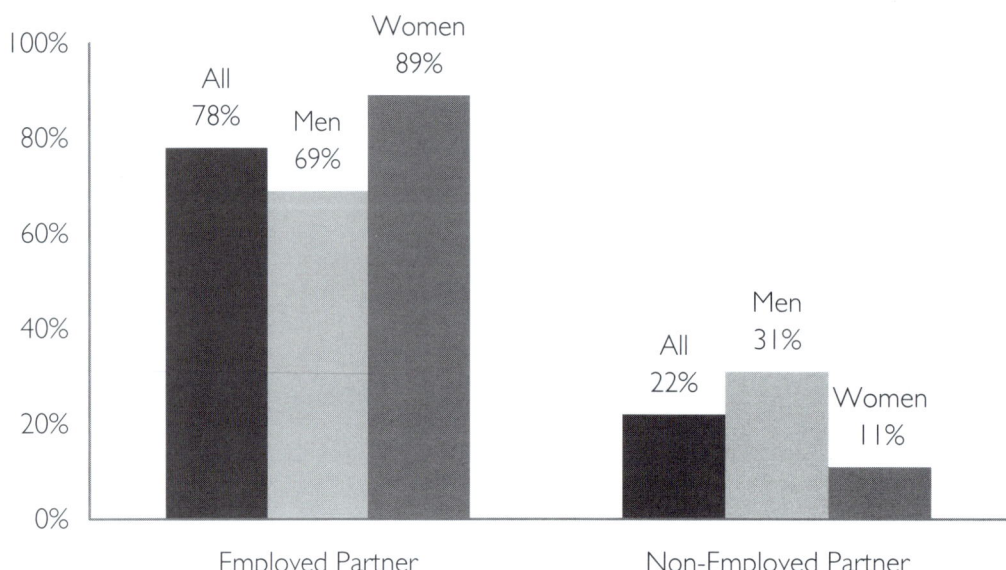

On average, employees in dual-earner couples work about 46 hours per week including both paid and unpaid time at their main jobs and any other jobs they have. In three-quarters of dual-earner households, both members of the couple work full-time.

- Considering all hours worked at all jobs as reported by the partner interviewed, one finds that in 75 percent of dual-earner households, both members of the couple work full-time.

- Although employees in dual-earner couples average 46.1 paid and unpaid hours per week at all paid jobs, men in dual-earner couples estimate they work 50.2 hours in total, while women estimate they work 42.4 hours per week in total, nearly eight fewer hours than men (Table 3.3). This discrepancy is due in part to the fact that more women work part time.

- Considering only employees in dual-earner couples whose main (only) job is full-time job (i.e., 35 or more scheduled hours per week), one finds the gap between men and women narrows from eight hours per week to about four hours per week, counting all paid and unpaid hours worked at all jobs.

- Among employees in dual-earner couples with children under 18, the gap widens to about 10 hours per week, with men working a total of 50.5 hours and women a total of 40.6 hours.

Table 3.3: Work Hours of Employees in Dual-Earner Couples

Paid and Unpaid Hours Worked Per Week at All Jobs	Mean *(sample size)*
All Employees in Dual-Earner Couples:	46.1 hours *(n=1436)*
Men	50.2 hours
Women	42.4 hours
Employees in Dual-Earner Couples Whose Main (Only) Job Is Full-time *(35 or more hours per week)*:	48.9 hours *(n=1245)*
Men	50.9 hours
Women	46.7 hours
Employees in Dual-Earner Couples with Children Under 18 at Home:	45.4 hours *(n=832)*
Men	50.5 hours
Women	40.6 hours

Today's average commute to and from work is more than three-quarters of an hour.

- The average of amount of time that employees spend each day getting to and from work is 47.5 minutes.

How Married Employees With Children Spend Their Time Off The Job

Although questions about "home chores" and "free-time activities" were asked of all employees, we limit the findings presented here to employed parents who were also asked questions about time spent "caring for and doing things with children." We further restricted the sample to employed married parents who have the potential to share responsibilities with their partners. Married parents include employees who are either legally married or living with a partner in a marriage-like relationship. We use the general term *partner* to refer both to spouses and partners.

It is important to note that, on average, married fathers work significantly longer hours (50.8) than mothers (40.4)—about 10 more hours per week considering all jobs. Because of their longer hours on the job, fathers presumably have fewer hours off the job than mothers to devote to family and personal activities—about 2 hours less per workday for those working a five-day week.

Our questions, which are identical to those used in the 1977 QES, ask respondents to estimate the amount of time they spent engaged in three broadly defined activities on the *average workday* and the *average day off work*. The amounts of time spent doing household chores and caring for and doing things with children may be, to some degree, overlapping. That is, a parent may be cooking dinner and helping a child with homework at the same time. Thus, time spent on chores and time with children should not be added together to estimate time engaged in unpaid work.

As with all research that does not use direct observation by researchers, responses may be biased by respondents' views of what is socially desirable. Indeed, other research[10] suggests that people's global estimates of time are likely to be upwardly biased—that is, higher than the actual amounts of time they spend in particular activities. However, estimates have been shown to be correlated with actual amounts of time spent and to be indicative of the relative amounts of time allocated to different activities. Thus, the comparisons presented in this section are best viewed as estimates of the *relative*, rather than *absolute*, amounts of time a spent by mothers and fathers at the same point in time as well as at different points in time.

When comparing data from 1997 with data from 1977, the 1997 NSCW sample is reduced to parents working 20 or more hours per week and interviewed in English to match the 1977 sample. In addition, the 1977 QES sample is reduced to parents 18 years and older to match the 1997 sample. Means for the full 1997 sample (column charts) may differ slightly from means for the reduced 1997 sample in comparisons with 1977 (line graphs).

Time Spent Caring for and Doing Things With Children

Among married parents, mothers spend more time caring for and doing things with their children on workdays and days off than fathers.

- Married mothers report spending nearly an hour more than fathers each workday "caring for and doing things with" their children (3.2 vs. 2.3 hours), as shown in Figure 3.8.

- On days off, the difference grows to nearly two hours per day, with mothers spending 8.3 hours and fathers 6.4 hours.

---

10. Robinson, J.P. and Godbey, G. (1997). *Time for Life: The Surprising Ways Americans Use Their Time.* University Park: The Pennsylvania State University Press.

Figure 3.8: Total Time Caring for and Doing Things with Children in 1997—Married Employees with Children (Hrs/Day)

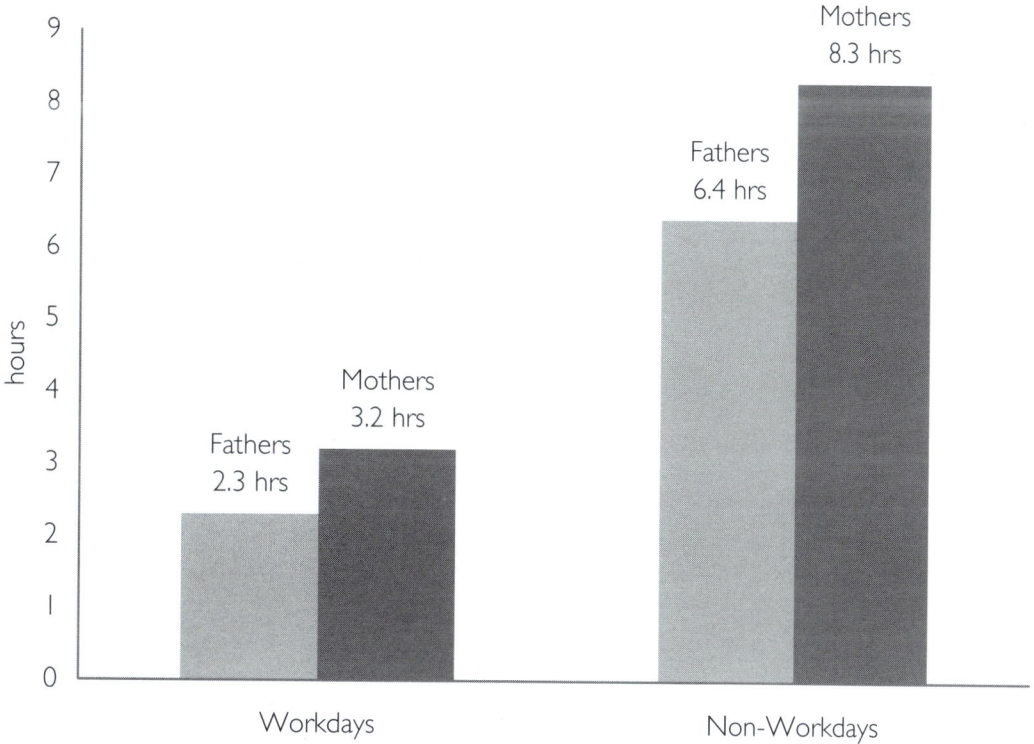

Having an employed partner makes no difference in the amount of time men spend with their children.

- The findings reported in Figure 3.8 (above) apply to employed married men whether they live in dual-earner or single-earner couples.

The question of whether employed mothers in dual-earner couples spend less time on child care than those with non-employed partners could not be reliably addressed with a sample of the size we are using, because there are so few employed married mothers in the U.S. labor force who have non-employed partners.

Although married fathers spend less time caring for and doing things with their children than mothers on *workdays*, the gap appears to have narrowed over the past 20 years.

- As shown in Figure 3.9, the workday time fathers report spending with their children has increased by 0.5 hours (30 minutes per workday) since 1977.

- There is no *significant* change from 1977 to 1997 in the *total* amount of time employed married mothers spend caring for and doing things with their children—about three hours per workday. Nor has the average time that mothers spent *per child* increased—2.0 hours in 1977 and 2.1 hours in 1997. Employed mothers have preserved the time they have with their children on workdays despite putting in longer hours on average at paid jobs.

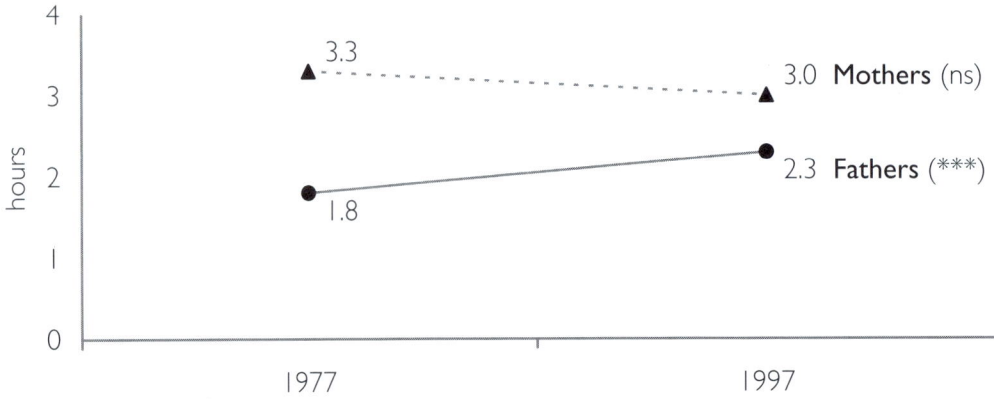

Figure 3.9: Workday Time for Children in 1977 and 1997— Married Employees with Children (Hrs/Day)

Significance: ns = not significant; *** = p < .0001

For purposes of comparison, the 1997 sample was reduced to employees working 20 or more hours per week and interviewed in English, while the 1977 sample was reduced to employees 18 and older. Means for the 1997 full and reduced samples may differ slightly.

Comparisons between 1997 and 1977 reveal that the *total* time married fathers spend with their children on *days off work* has also increased, while mothers' time has remained the same.

- Among married employees with children, the time fathers spend caring for and doing things with their children increased significantly by slightly more than one hour per non-workday (Figure 3.10).

- Although employed married mothers' time increased by about the same *absolute* amount from 1977 to 1997, this difference did not reach statistical significance, mainly because of the small number of employed married mothers in the 1977 sample.

However, 20-year comparisons did reveal significant increases in the hours that both married mothers and fathers spend *per child* on days off work.

- The time spent *per child* on days off work increased by 0.4 hours for fathers and 1.2 hours for married mothers over the past 20 years, a period during which the average number of children per family has declined.

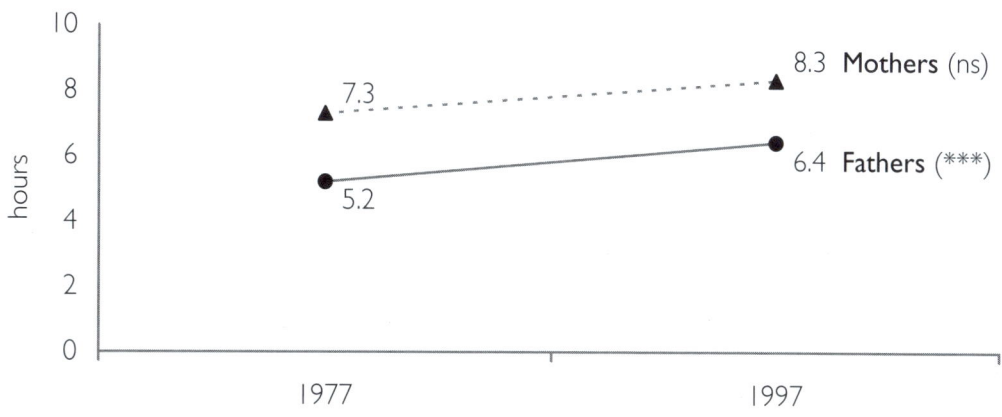

Figure 3.10: Total Non-Workday Time for Children in 1977 and 1997— Married Employees with Children (Hrs/Day)

Significance: ns = not significant; *** = p < .0001

For purposes of comparison, the 1997 sample was reduced to employees working 20 or more hours per week and interviewed in English, while the 1977 sample was reduced to employees 18 and older. Means for the 1997 full and reduced samples may differ slightly.

Children appear to be receiving somewhat more attention from their employed parents today than was the case 20 years ago.

- Overall, children appear to receive somewhat more attention from their employed parents today than 20 years ago. Based on self-reports, married fathers have increased the *total* amount of time they spend with their children on workdays and days off work, and mothers have managed to at least preserve the amount of time they spend with their children on workdays despite working longer hours. Although *total* time with children on days off work did not increase significantly for mothers, time *per child* on days off work did increase for both mothers and fathers, who have somewhat fewer children

> The amount of time that married mothers spend with their children on workdays has remained steady over the past 20 years—despite their longer hours at paid jobs.

41 *Life Off the Job*

today than employed parents did in 1977. Our findings do not, however, address the questions of whether the *content* of the time that children and parents spend together has changed for better or worse over the past 20 years, whether fathers and mothers engage in the same kinds of activities with their children, or whether mothers still have primary responsibility for ensuring that the full range of children's needs are met.

Among married parents, a majority of mothers and more than two in five fathers would like their partners to spend more time with their children. In addition, 70 percent of parents—mothers and fathers—feel they do not have enough time to spend with their children.

- Married mothers (56 percent) are more likely than fathers (43 percent) to wish their partners would spend more time with their children, but both proportions are large.

- Overall, 70 percent of mothers and fathers feel they do not have enough time to spend with their children.

> Overall, 70 percent of employed mothers and fathers feel they do not have enough time to spend with their children.

To some extent, the first finding may reflect judgments that partners are not carrying equal or appropriate parenting loads. However, the second finding suggests that the primary basis for both findings may be that individual married parents wish both they and their partners could spend more time with their children.

Time on Household Chores

"Home chores" were defined as "things like cooking, cleaning, repairs, shopping, yardwork, and keeping track of money and bills."

Among married parents, mothers spend more time than men on home chores, both on workdays and on days when they are not working.

- As shown in Figure 3.11, married mothers report spending 1 hour more than fathers doing household chores on the average workday and on the average day off work.

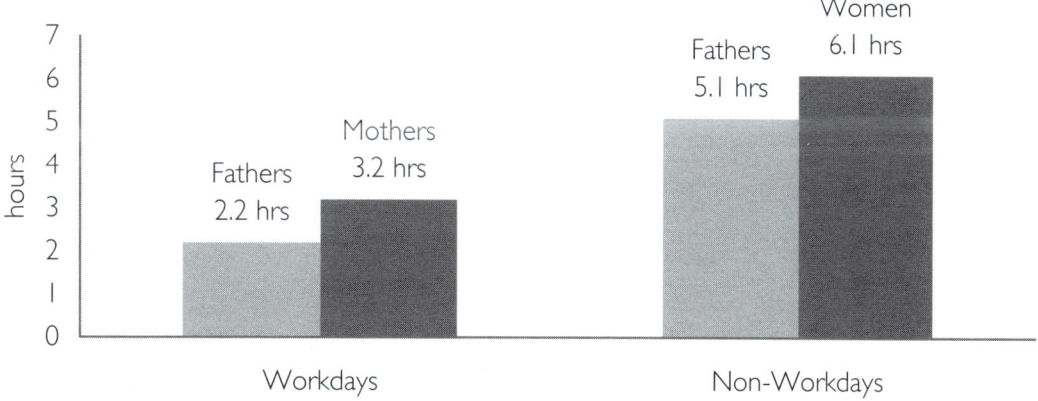

Figure 3.11: Time on Chores in 1997—Married Employees with Children (Hrs/Day)

Although married mothers spend more time than fathers doing chores on both workdays and non-workdays, this gap has narrowed substantially over the past 20 years.

- As shown in Figure 3.12, the difference between the time fathers and married mothers spend doing chores on workdays was much greater in 1977 (2.5 hours per day) than it is in 1997 (0.9 hours per day). Put differently, fathers spent 32 percent as much time on workday chores as mothers did in 1977 compared with 71 percent as much time today.

- The workday time mothers spend on chores declined significantly from 1977 to 1997 by 36 minutes per day, while the time men spend increased significantly by 1 hour per day.

Figure 3.12: Workday Time on Chores in 1977 and 1997—
Married Employees with Children (Hrs/Day)

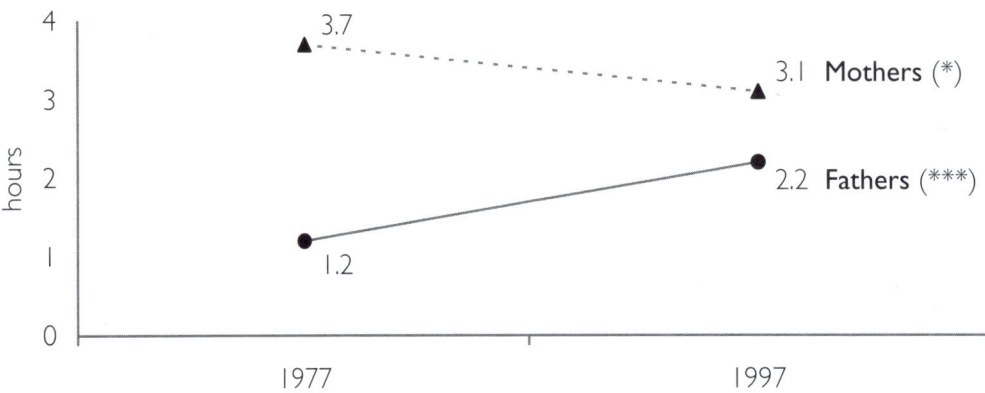

Significance: * = p < .01 *** = p < .0001

For purposes of comparison, the 1997 sample was reduced to employees working 20 or more hours per week and interviewed in English, while the 1977 sample was reduced to employees 18 and older. Means for the 1997 full and reduced samples may differ slightly.

Similarly, differences between the time married mothers and fathers spend doing chores on days off work have decreased substantially from 1977 to 1997.

- As shown in Figure 3.13, the difference between the time married fathers and mothers spend doing chores on days off was much greater in 1977 (3 hours per day) than it is in 1997 (1 hour per day). In 1977, fathers spent 58 percent as much time as mothers on non-workdays compared with 84 percent today.

- The non-workday time women spend on chores declined significantly from 1977 to 1997 by 1.1 hours per day, while the time men spend increased significantly by a nearly equal amount—0.9 hours (54 minutes) per day.

> The non-workday time married mothers spend on chores declined significantly from 1977 to 1997 by 1 hour per day, while the time fathers spend increased significantly by a nearly equal amount.

Life Off the Job

Figure 3.13: Non-Workday Time on Chores in 1977 and 1997—Married Employees with Children (Hrs/Day)

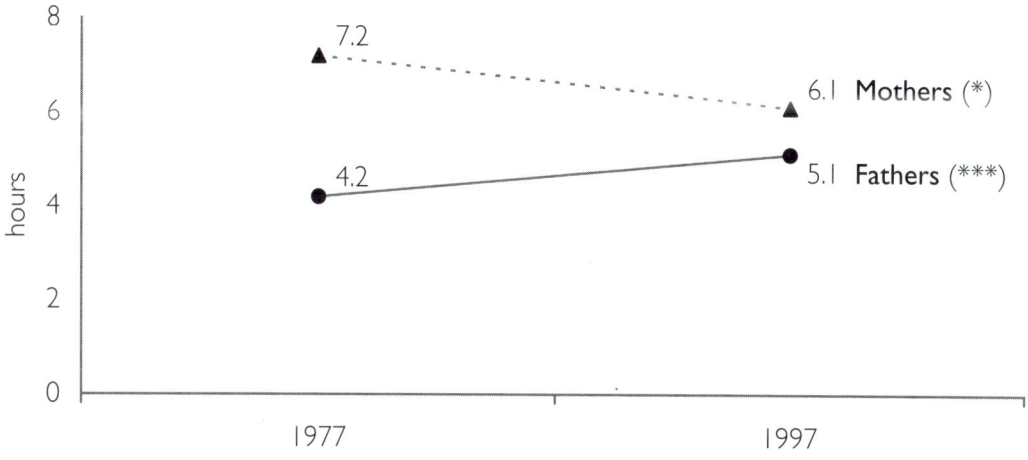

Significance: * = p < .01; *** = p < .0001

For purposes of comparison, the 1997 sample was reduced to employees working 20 or more hours per week and interviewed in English, while the 1977 sample was reduced to employees 18 and older. Means for the 1997 full and reduced samples may differ slightly.

Despite the substantial increase over the past 20 years in the time married fathers spend doing household chores, one-half of married mothers want their partners to spend more time on chores.

- Among married parents, 50 percent of mothers want their partners to spend even more time on household chores than they currently spend. In contrast, only 18 percent of fathers want their partners to spend more time on chores.

Unfortunately, comparable data are not available from 1977 to determine whether mothers' and fathers' expectations of their partners have changed in recent years. Nor do we know the specific content of the chores performed by mothers and fathers or who makes sure vital tasks get done.

Time for Personal Activities

The interviews conducted in the 1997 National Study of the Changing Workforce and the 1977 Quality of Employment Survey did not ask about *leisure time* in general, which might well include time spent doing things with children, but more specifically about time spent engaged in "your own free-time activities," which is less likely to include time with children. We use the terms *personal activities*, *personal time*, and *time for self* interchangeably when referring to employees' *own free-time activities*.

Married fathers spend more time than mothers engaged in personal activities on both workdays and days off.

- On average, married fathers reporting having 1.2 hours for themselves on workdays, while mothers have 0.9 hours—a difference of 18 minutes per day.

- Although both mothers and fathers have substantially more time for personal activities on days off work, fathers spend nearly an hour more engaged in personal activities on days off work than mothers—3.4 versus 2.5 hours per non-workday.

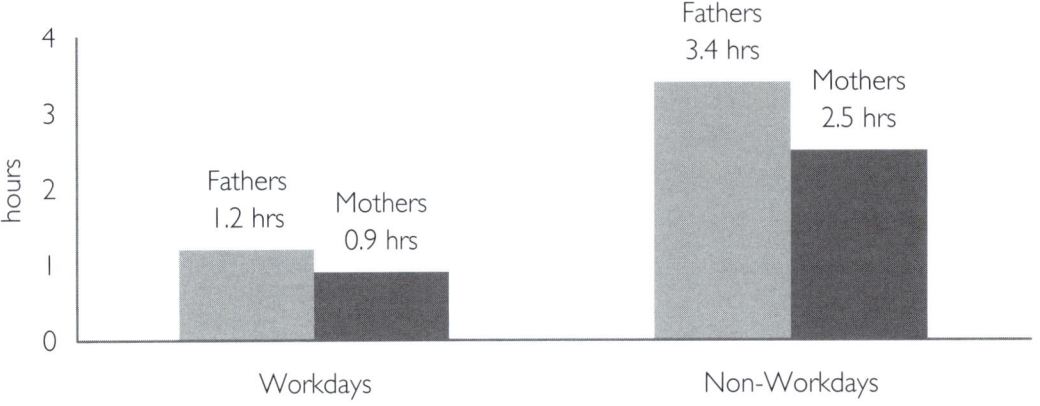

Figure 3.14: Time for Personal Activities in 1997—Married Employees with Children (Hrs/Day)

Married parents—both men and women—have much less time for themselves than married employees without children do.

- Married fathers have an hour less per workday of personal time than non-fathers do—1.2 versus 2.2 hours per workday. Fathers have more than two hours less for themselves on days off work than non-fathers do—3.4 versus 5.7 hours.

- Similarly, married mothers have nearly an hour less than women without children for personal activities on workdays—0.9 versus 1.8 hours. On days off work, mothers have nearly three hours less for themselves than non-mothers do—2.5 versus 5.3 hours.

> Married fathers spend an hour less engaged in personal activities on workdays than married men without children—1.2 versus 2.2 hours.

Over the past 20 years, the amount of workday time married mothers and fathers have for their own personal activities has declined.

- On average, married fathers in 1997 have 54 fewer minutes for themselves on workdays than fathers 20 years ago did, while mothers have 42 fewer minutes for themselves on workdays today than mothers in 1977 (Figure 3.15) did.

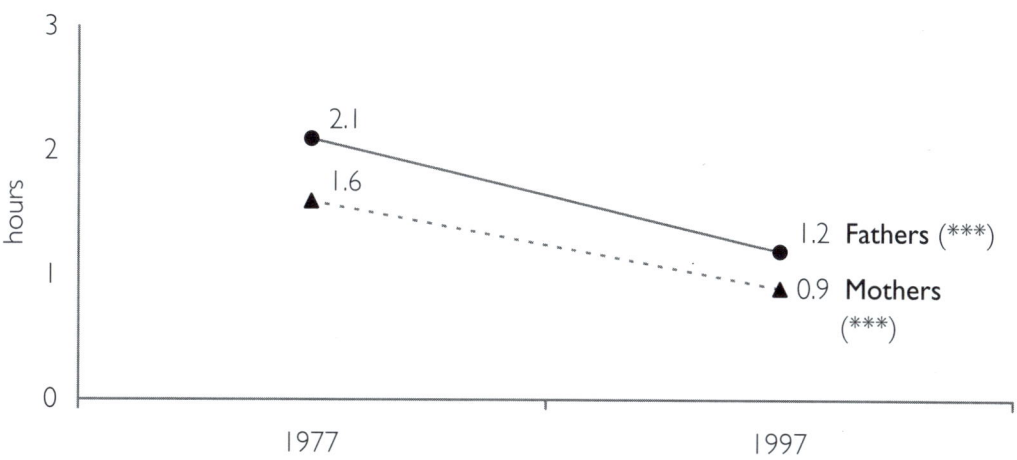

Figure 3.15: Workday Time for Self in 1977 and 1997—Married Employees with Children (Hrs/Day)

Significance: *** = p < .0001

For purposes of comparison, the 1997 sample was reduced to employees working 20 or more hours per week and interviewed in English, while the 1977 sample was reduced to employees 18 and older. Means for the 1997 full and reduced samples may differ slightly.

The time both married fathers and mothers engage in personal activities on days off work has also declined over the past 20 years.

- Fathers' time for themselves on days off work has decreased from 5.1 to 3.3 hours on days when they are not working—a change of 1.8 hours. Mothers' time for themselves on days off has declined from 3.3 hours to 2.5 hours—a change of 0.8 hours over the past 20 years.

- While mothers reported having only 65 percent of the free time that fathers had in 1977, today the time they have for themselves is 76 percent of that reported by fathers. However, this apparent convergence toward gender equity is a very mixed blessing since both mothers and fathers report having substantially less time for themselves than 20 years ago.

Figure 3.16: Non-Workday Time for Self in 1977 and 1997—Married Employees with Children (Hrs/Day)

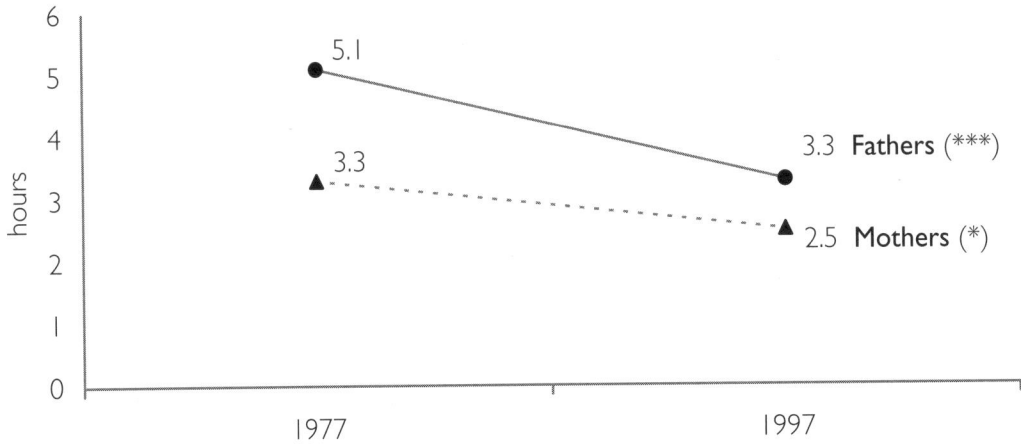

Significance: * = p < .01; *** = p < .0001

For purposes of comparison, the 1997 sample was reduced to employees working 20 or more hours per week and interviewed in English, while the 1977 sample was reduced to employees 18 and older. Means for the 1997 full and reduced samples may differ slightly.

Discussion of Findings

What conclusions can be reached based on the findings presented in this section? Are married fathers really assuming more responsibility for child care and household work? Is our society approaching gender equity on the home front?

Any conclusion should be qualified, particularly since our findings appear to contradict at least some of the conclusions reached by other researchers and their interpreters. Drawing upon extensive and detailed time-diary data from 1965, 1975, and 1985, Robinson and Godbey[11] report that time doing "core housework" increased for employed men and decreased for employed women from 1965 through 1985 and that time devoted to "child care" did not increase for either employed fathers or mothers over the same period. They also report that "free time" increased for employed men and women.

Unfortunately our findings and their findings are not directly comparable. First, in this section we analyze data only for employed men and women who are both parents and married—a subsample of the labor force for which Robinson (to our knowledge) has not

---

11. Robinson, J.P. and Godbey, G. (1997). *Time for Life: The Surprising Ways Americans Use Their Time.* University Park: The Pennsylvania State University Press.

published findings. Second, Robinson's most recently published findings are based on 1985 data collected 12 years before the 1997 NSCW data used in this report. Third, our activity categories are much broader than his and are reported for workdays and non-workdays rather than weeks. We hope that more comparable findings from his 1995 survey will be forthcoming.

We are most confident of our findings about decreases mothers' time and increases fathers' time doing household chores on workdays and days off work over the past 20 years, since they are statistically robust and apparently consistent with other research. It remains to be seen whether our findings of marked declines in married mothers' and fathers' time for themselves—with possible convergence of fathers' and mothers' personal time on days off work—will be supported by other research.

Most controversial is our finding that the time employed married fathers report spending with their children on workdays and days off work has increased over the past 20 years, while employed married mothers' time has remained the same. Are fathers more prone to exaggeration about their involvement in child care than mothers? Our 1997 data provide a reality check of sorts. Married mothers were asked how much time their partners spent caring for and doing things with children on workdays and days off work. Interviewed mothers' estimates for their partners (a random sample of all male employees in dual-earner couples with children in the labor force) do not differ significantly from the self-reports of interviewed fathers (also a random sample of all male employees in dual-earner couples with children in the labor force). Mothers, at least, do not appear to think fathers are exaggerating.

In sum, married parents appear to be dividing the family workload somewhat more evenly today than 20 years ago. To what extent such changes are driven by necessity (as employed mothers spend longer hours at paid work and fewer relatives are available to provide low- or no-cost child care) or by changing attitudes and values has not been determined. However, it seems likely that both necessity and changing values have an influence.

A final caveat: Time spent performing a task does not necessarily equal responsibility assumed for the task. Findings from our 1992 survey[12] indicated that women in dual-earner couples—according to both men and women—were much more likely than their partners to have primary responsibility for cooking, cleaning, shopping, and child care. Whether responsibilities for planning and overseeing family work are being divided more equally today than 5 or 20 years ago cannot be addressed with data from the 1997 NSCW or 1977 QES.

---

12. Galinsky, E., Bond, J.T., & Friedman, D.E. (1993). *The Changing Workforce: Highlights of the National Study.* New York: Families and Work Institute.

Child and Elder Care Responsibilities

Among all employed parents with pre-kindergarten children, the most frequent child care arrangement for their youngest child is care by family members, but the number relying upon non-family arrangements is also substantial.

- Overall, 47 percent of employed parents—including those with employed partners as well as those whose partners are not employed—rely on their partners as the main source of care for their youngest pre-kindergarten children while they are working. An additional 19 percent depend on their relatives. Center-based care is the choice of 20 percent, while non-relative care in the non-relative's home (family child care) or in the child's home accounts for the remaining 13 percent (Table 3.4).

Table 3.4: Care Arrangements for Youngest Child Not Yet in School

Arrangements	Percentage *(sample size)*
All Workers:	*(n=449)*
Main Type of Child Care Arrangement for Youngest Child Not in School:	
Parental care	47%
Center care	20
Relative care	19
Non-relative care	13
Parental Care by Gender:	
Employed fathers' reliance on care by partner	66%
Employed mother's reliance on care by partner	22%
Dual Earners:	*(n=274)*
Main Type of Child Care Arrangement for Youngest Child Not in School	
Parental care	35%
Center care	27
Relative care	20
Non-relative care	19
Parental Care by Gender:	
Employed fathers' reliance on care by partner	48%
Employed mother's reliance on care by partner	24%

- Reliance upon parental care drops to 35 percent among employees in dual-earner couples, but remains surprisingly high, revealing the lengths to which some employed parents go to address primary child care needs within their immediate families by adjusting work schedules. Reliance on relative care remains the same, while use of center and non-relative care rises correspondingly.

Employed mothers are much less likely than employed fathers to rely on their partners as the primary source of child care for their pre-kindergarten children during work hours.

- Among all employed parents with pre-kindergarten children, mothers are much less likely (22 percent) than fathers (66 percent) to rely on their partners to provide child care during work hours.

- This gap narrows substantially among dual-earner couples, mainly as a result of differences in child care arrangements among fathers. Twenty-four percent of mothers and 48 percent of fathers in dual-earner couples rely on their partners as the primary source of care for their youngest pre-kindergarten child during work hours. Nonetheless, even in dual-earner couples, reliance on parental care remains quite high.

Twenty-nine percent of employed parents have had to make other arrangements one or more times in the past three months because their regular child care was unavailable. Those experiencing the fewest child care breakdowns use center-based or parental child care.

- On average, employed parents must make special arrangements about once every three months because their usual child care is not available.

> Reliance upon parental care among employees in dual-earner couples remains surprisingly high, revealing the lengths to which some employed parents go to address primary child care needs within their immediate families by adjusting work schedules.

Life Off the Job

Table 3.5: Child Care Breakdowns

Child Care Breakdowns	Percentage or Mean (sample size)
All Workers with Children Less Than 13:	(n=981)
Mean number of child care breakdowns in past 3 months	0.9
Frequency distribution by category:	
None	71%
1-2 times	18
3 or more	11
Mean Number of Child Care Breakdowns Crossed with Main Type of Child Care:	*** [P&C<R&N]
Parental care (P)	0.5
Center care (C)	0.8
Relative care (R)	1.6
Non-relative care (N)	1.7

Significance: *** = $p < .0001$

- Employed parents who leave their children with the other parent or at a child care center while at work experience significantly fewer child care breakdowns than parents who leave their children with a relative or in non-relative care (Table 3.5).

> When one member of a dual-earner couple has to care for a sick child or attend to other needs of children when both are supposed to be on the job, employed mothers are much more likely than fathers to assume this responsibility.

- Married fathers in dual-earner couples report that their partners are more likely (69 percent) than they are to take time off work to attend to their children's needs, while 22 percent say they are more likely to miss work, and 9 percent say "it depends."

- Eighty-three percent of employed mothers feel they are more likely than their spouses/partners to miss work for child-related reasons—a higher proportion than indicated by the responses of working fathers. Moreover, only 10 percent of employed mothers report that their partners are more likely than they are to take time off to attend to their children's needs.

Eighty-three percent of employed mothers feel they are more likely than their spouses/partners to miss work for child-related reasons.

Rather than speculating about whose views are more objective, we simply conclude that by all accounts employed mothers in dual-earner couples are given and/or take greater responsibility than their partners for addressing children's needs during regular work hours. We also find that employed mothers in dual-earner couples are somewhat more likely to be absent from work because of providing sick-child care—2.8 days per year—than men in dual-earner couples—0.9 days per year.

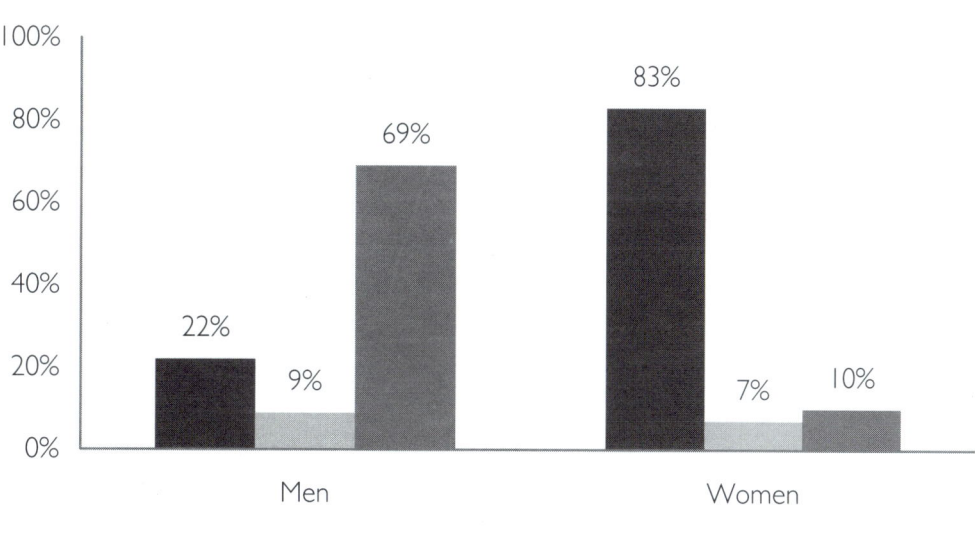

Figure 3.17: Dual Earner Couples: Who is more likely to take time off work to attend to children's needs?

One out of four wage and salaried workers provided assistance to an elderly family member during the past year, and more than a third took time away from work to do so. Moreover, one in five employees with children also had elder responsibilities during the preceding year.

Elder care findings are discussed at greater length in Chapter 9 of the report and so will not be elaborated here.

Attitudes Toward Working Women and Mothers

Two out of five employees—both men and women—think it's much better if men are the breadwinners and women take care of the home and children. And fully one-half of employed married women with children feel that it's better for women to be at home.

- Forty-one percent of employees in 1997 agree with the following statement: "It is much better for everyone involved if the man earns the money and the woman takes care of the home and children." There is no statistically significant difference between men and women (Figure 3.18).

- Moreover, there are no differences in the attitudes of employed men and women who are married and have children, as also shown in Figure 3.18. However, the overall proportion agreeing that "it's much better for everyone involved if the man earns the money and the woman takes care of the home and children" increases to 49 percent among married employees with children, compared with 41 percent for all workers.

These findings strongly suggest that many married employees are ambivalent about mothers working outside the home. Efforts to balance commitments to children and partners, the economic benefits of having two earners, the need to develop and maintain a profile of employability in a world where half of all marriages end in divorce and partners may lose their jobs in downsizing, and the desire to pursue a personally gratifying career all create enormous tensions for married employees today. Satisfactory resolution of these tensions may well require the involvement of employers, communities, and government, as well as employees themselves.

Figure 3.18: Percentage Agreeing That It Is Better for Man to Earn Money and Woman to Care for Home and Children

Two-thirds of employees think employed mothers can have relationships with their children that are just as good as those of stay-at-home mothers. However, employed men are less likely than employed women to feel this way.

- Overall, 67 percent of wage and salaried workers in 1997 agreed with the following statement: "A mother who works outside the home can have just as good a relationship with her children as a mother who does not work." As shown in Figure 3.19, employed women are more likely to agree (73 percent) than employed men (62 percent).

- The firsthand experience of being a parent does not appear to affect these attitudes.

Figure 3.19: Percentage Agreeing That a Working Mother Can Have As Good a Relationship with Her Children as a Non-Working Mother, 1997

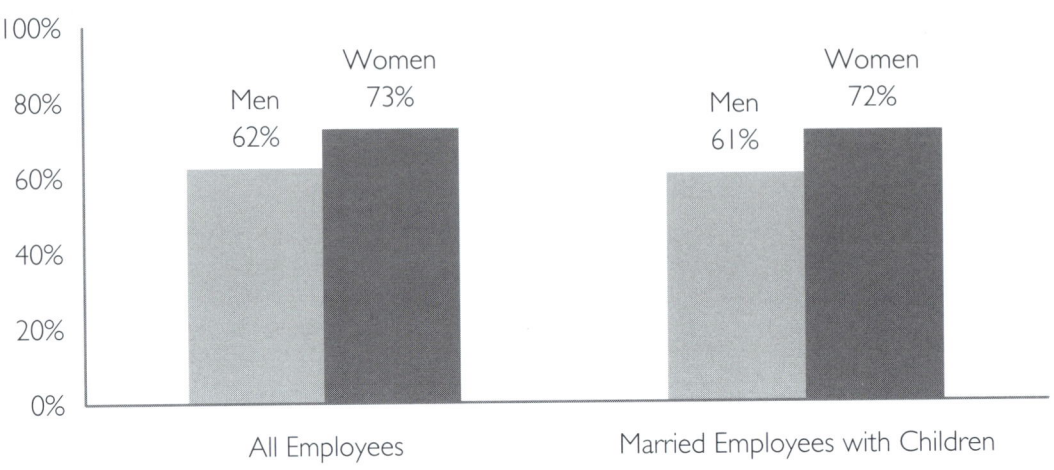

Attitudes toward working women's and mothers' participation in the labor force have become much more favorable over the past 20 years.

- Since 1977 there has been a decrease of 23 percentage points—from 64 percent to 41 percent—in the proportion of wage and salaried workers who think men should be the breadwinners and women should care for the home and children.[13] To what extent this reflects cultural change or growing economic pressures on families is an unresolved issue.

- A higher proportion of today's workers (67 percent) than workers in 1977 (58 percent) also believe that employed mothers can have relationships with their children that are just as good as the relationships non-employed mothers have.

> Since 1977 there has been a decrease of 23 percentage points—from 64 percent to 41 percent—in the proportion of wage and salaried workers who think men should be the breadwinners and women should care for the home and children.

---

13. For purposes of comparison, the 1997 sample was reduced to employees working 20 or more hours per week and interviewed in English, while the 1977 sample was reduced to employees 18 and older. Percentages for the 1997 full and reduced samples may differ slightly.

4 Personal Well-Being

Employees' personal well-being is not only a matter of individual concern, but is also important to children, families, communities, and business. The findings presented in this chapter reveal that many employees are stressed, have trouble coping, are not satisfied with their lives, feel burned out by their jobs, and experience negative spillover from their jobs into their personal lives. As Chapter 8 will show, employees whose personal well-being is impaired by their jobs also exhibit lower job performance. Research by others indicates that the personal well-being of employees is related to effective parenting, healthy child development, and the costs of medical care, which are largely covered by employers.

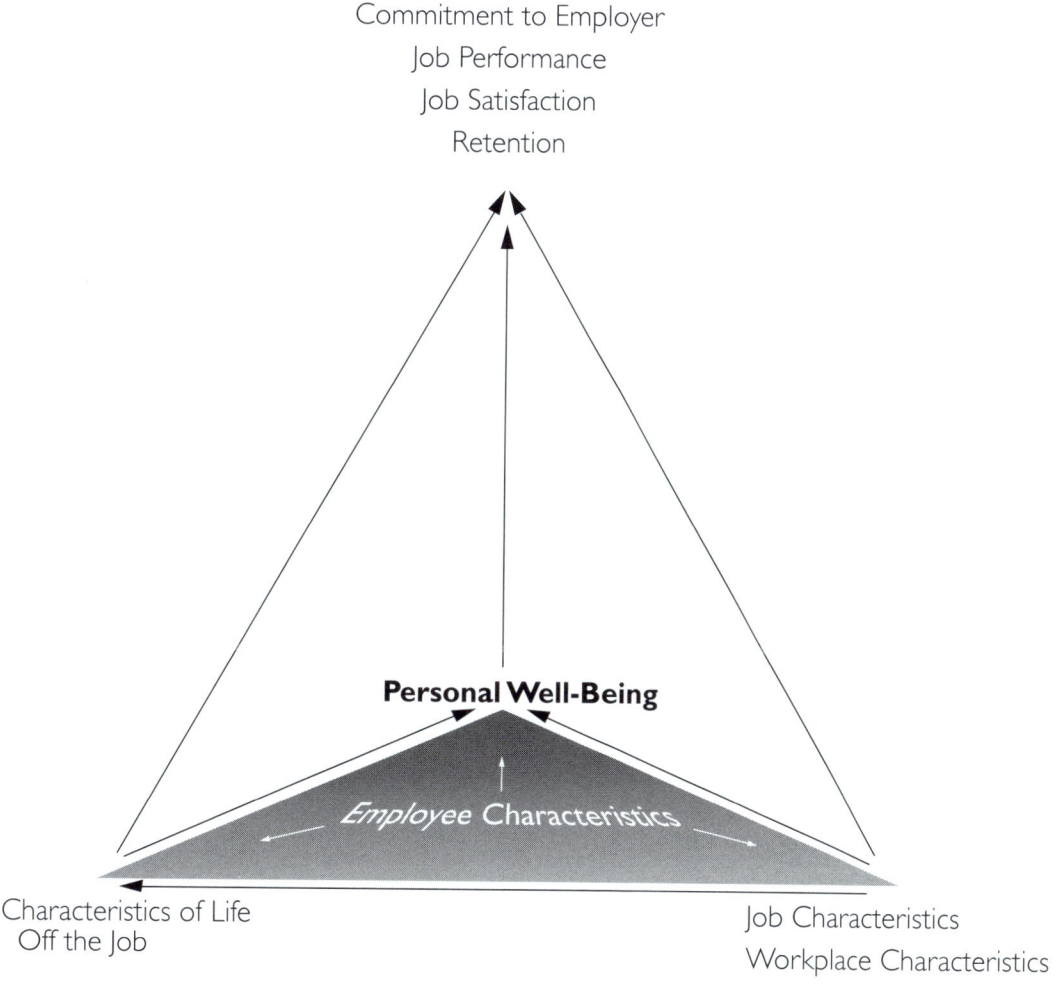

57 *Personal Well-Being*

Fifteen questions provide measures of personal well-being. They are divided into two categories: *general well-being* and *job-related well-being*. General well-being reflects employees' overall feelings of emotional health. Job-related well-being measures employees' perceptions of how their jobs affect their well-being off the job. Comparisons are made, as appropriate, with data from the 1992 survey.

General Well-Being

More than half of employees in 1997 have felt nervous or stressed sometimes or more often over the past three months—a slight decrease from 1992.

> Thirty-eight percent of employees say they are bothered sometimes or more often by minor health problems often associated with stress, such as headaches, insomnia, or stomach pains.

- Fifty-three percent of employees in 1997 report that they very often, often, or sometimes felt nervous or stressed during the three months prior to the interview (Figure 4.1)—five percentage points fewer than in 1992.

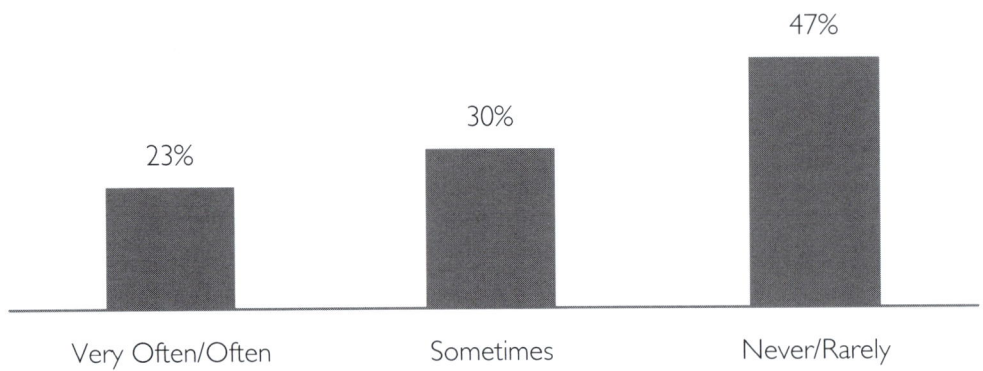

Figure 4.1: During the past three months, how often have you felt nervous or stressed?

- In addition, 38 percent say they are bothered sometimes or more often by minor health problems often associated with stress, such as headaches, insomnia, or stomach pains (Figure 4.2). The incidence of such physical symptoms is the same in 1997 as it was in 1992.

58 *Personal Well-Being*

Figure 4.2: How often are you bothered by minor health problems?

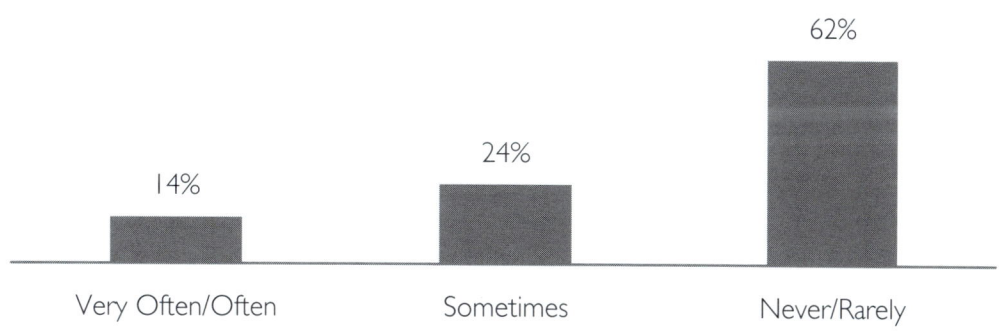

More than one-third of employees have had difficulty coping with the demands of everyday life sometimes or more often in the past three months—no more or less than employees surveyed five years ago.

- Thirty-five percent of all workers report that during the three months prior to the interview they sometimes or more often experienced periods when they could not cope with all the things they needed to do. Findings for 1997 do not differ from those obtained in 1992.

Figure 4.3: In the past three months, how often have you not been able to cope with all the things you have to do?

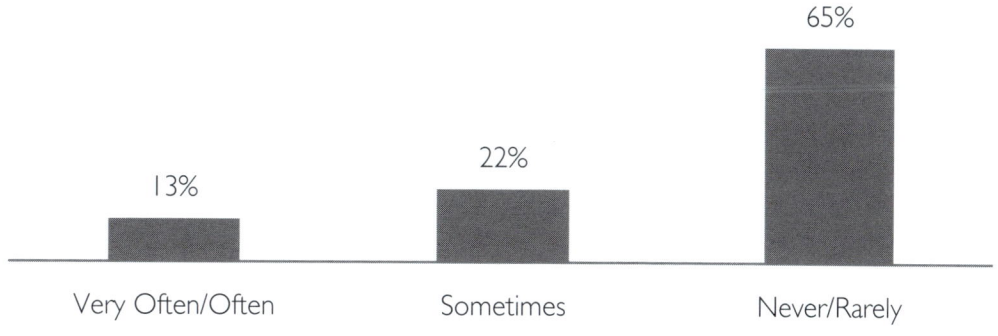

Most employees are relatively satisfied with their lives in general, their family lives, and their relationships with their partners, but many have reservations.

- Eighty-six percent of employees feel somewhat or very satisfied with their lives in general. This percentage has not changed in the past five years. However, employees who are very satisfied with their lives are a minority—33 percent—of all workers.

- Among employees living with partners or children, 31 percent are extremely satisfied with their family lives, while 38 percent are very satisfied, 27 percent are somewhat satisfied, and 2 percent are not too satisfied.

- Among employees who are legally married or living with a partner, 51 percent feel extremely satisfied with that relationship and another 34 percent feel very satisfied. Fifteen percent are only somewhat satisfied or not too satisfied.

Satisfaction with family life has declined over the past 20 years.

- On average, satisfaction with family life has decreased over the past 20 years. While the proportions of *married employees with children*[1] who are extremely satisfied and not too satisfied—the two ends of the response continuum—has remained the same since 1977, the proportion who are very satisfied has dropped from 55 to 39 percent, and the proportion who are only somewhat satisfied has increased from 15 to 28 percent.

- Satisfaction with life in general has not changed since 1992, our only historical point of comparison, nor has marital satisfaction changed since 1977.

> Eighty-six percent of employees feel somewhat or very satisfied with their lives in general. This percentage has not changed in the past five years. Employees who are very satisfied with their lives are a minority—33 percent—of all workers.

---

1. In the 1977 QES, this question was only asked of married employees with children.

Table 4.1: Employees' General Feelings of Satisfaction

Satisfaction	Percentage (sample size)
General Life Satisfaction:	(n=2868)
All things considered, how do you feel about your life these days?	
Very dissatisfied	2%
Somewhat dissatisfied	12
Somewhat satisfied	53
Very satisfied	33
Satisfaction with Family Life:	(n=2428)
All in all, how satisfied are you with your family life?	
Not too satisfied	3%
Somewhat dissatisfied	27
Very satisfied	38
Extremely satisfied	31
Satisfaction with Marital Life:	(n=1850)
All in all, how satisfied are you with your marriage/relationship?	
Not too satisfied	2%
Somewhat satisfied	13
Very satisfied	34
Extremely satisfied	51

Married employees feel somewhat more satisfied with their lives in general than single employees; however, they do not experience any less stress or cope more effectively.

- Eighty-nine percent of married employees feel somewhat or very satisfied with their lives, while 81 percent of single workers feel the same—a significant difference. However, married and single employees do not differ with respect to their feelings of stress and nervousness; 23 percent of both groups have felt stressed or nervous often or very often in the past three months. Nor do they differ in their ability to cope with life demands.

Employees in dual-earner couples feel more stressed and have somewhat greater difficulty coping than married employees in single-earner families.

- Employees who have employed partners report feeling more nervous and stressed than employees with partners who are not employed. Nearly one-quarter (23 percent) of workers with employed partners, versus 15 percent of workers in single-earner couples, felt nervous or stressed very often or often in the three months prior to the interview.

- Similarly, workers with employed partners are slightly more likely (13 percent) than workers with partners who are not employed (9 percent) to say they often or very often could not cope with everything they needed to do.

- Although workers with employed partners feel more stressed and less able to cope than married coworkers with non-employed partners, both groups feel equally satisfied with their lives—with 89 percent responding that they feel somewhat or very satisfied.

Employees with children under 18 are no more likely than employees without children to feel stressed or have trouble coping, and both groups are equally satisfied with their lives in general.

Job-Related Well-Being

Job and workplace factors can have significant effects on the quality of employees' personal lives and emotional health. We examine two measures of job-related well-being in this section: *job burnout* and *job-to-home spillover*. In both instances, we asked employees to assess the causal linkages between work life and personal life. Job burnout is measured by the four questions presented in Table 4.2. Job-to-home spillover is measured by the five questions presented in Table 4.3. Items were averaged to create job burnout and job-to-home spillover indices for use in data analysis.

One-quarter to more than one-third of employees experience some form of job-related stress often or very often.

- One in four employees (26 percent) report having felt "stressed and burned-out" or "emotionally drained" by work often or very often during the three months prior to the interview. And 36 percent often or very often felt "used up at the end of the workday" or "tired when [they] got up in the morning and had to face another day on the job." Another 31 to 35 percent of employees answered "sometimes" to these four questions. (Table 4.2)

- Women report slightly higher levels of job burnout than men on the overall index of burnout, which averages responses to the four questions. There is no difference on the job burnout index between workers with and those without children or between married employees with employed partners and those without employed partners.

Employees in 1997 feel slightly less burned-out by their jobs today than those interviewed five years ago.

- Using our overall index of job burnout, we find that job burnout has decreased slightly but significantly from 1992 to 1997.

Table 4.2: Employees' Feelings of Job Burnout

How often during the past three months…	NSCW 1997 Percentage *(sample size)*
…have you felt emotionally drained from your work?	*(n=2868)*
Never	16%
Rarely	25
Sometimes	32
Often	13
Very often	13
…have you felt used up at the end of the workday?	*(n=2873)*
Never	10%
Rarely	19
Sometimes	35
Often	19
Very often	17
…have you felt tired when you got up in the morning and had to face another day on the job?	*(n=2871)*
Never	10%
Rarely	23
Sometimes	32
Often	19
Very often	17

Table 4.2 (continued): Employees' Feelings of Job Burnout

... have you felt burned out or stressed by your work?	(n=2876)
Never	17%
Rarely	27
Sometimes	31
Often	14
Very often	12

One-quarter to more than one-third of employees experience negative spillover from their jobs into their personal lives often or very often.

From employees' perspectives, life on the job has direct effects on mood, energy level, and the amount and quality of time they have for family, friends, and themselves (Table 4.3).

- In the last three months:

    Twenty-six percent of employees felt they often or very often were not in as good a mood as they would have liked to have been at home because of their jobs; another 34 percent sometimes feel this way.

    Twenty-seven percent of employees felt they often or very often did not have enough time for their family or other important people in their lives because of their jobs; another 31 percent sometimes feel this way.

    Twenty-eight percent of employees felt they often or very often did not have enough energy to do things with their family or friends because of their jobs; another 29 percent sometimes feel this way.

    Thirty-two percent of employees felt they often or very often did not have enough time for themselves because of their jobs; another 33 percent sometimes feel this way.

    Thirty-five percent of employees felt they often or very often were not able to get everything done at home each day because of their jobs; another 30 percent sometimes feel this way.

- Employees' perceptions of the negative spillover from job-to-home in 1997 and in 1992 are not significantly different.

A very large proportion of U.S. employees experience negative spillover from their jobs to their personal lives, in one form or another and in varying degrees. Chapter 8 will explore the related consequences for performance on the job.

> Twenty-eight percent of employees felt they often or very often did not have enough energy to do things with their family or friends because of their jobs; another 29 percent sometimes feel this way.

Table 4.3: Prevalence of Negative Job-To-Home Spillover

In the past three months, how often have you...	Percentage (sample size)
... not had enough time for yourself because of your job?	(n=2867)
Never	13%
Rarely	23
Sometimes	33
Often	16
Very often	16
... not had enough time for your family or other important people in your life because of your job?	(n=2870)
Never	16%
Rarely	26
Sometimes	31
Often	15
Very often	12
... not had the energy to do things with your family or other important people in your life because of your job?	(n=2866)
Never	16%
Rarely	26
Sometimes	29
Often	16
Very often	12
... not been able to get everything done at home each day because of your job?	(n=2872)
Never	14%
Rarely	21
Sometimes	30
Often	20
Very often	15
... not been in as good a mood as you would like to be at home because of your job?	(n=2871)
Never	14%
Rarely	27
Sometimes	34
Often	15
Very often	11

Employed parents are more likely than other workers to feel they do not have enough energy or time to spend with family and friends or cannot get things done at home because of their jobs.

- Thirty-three percent of employed parents, compared with 23 percent of employees without children, often or very often feel they do not have enough time for friends and family because of their jobs (Figure 4.4).

Figure 4.4: How often have you not had enough time for your family or other important people in your life because of your job?

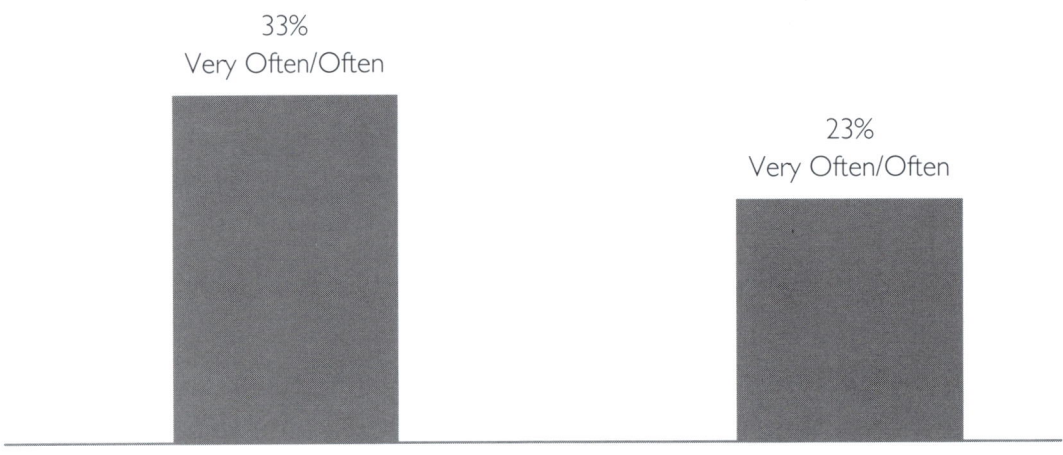

- Likewise, 32 percent of working parents have often or very often not had the energy to do things with their families or other important people in their lives, compared with 26 percent of employees without children.

- Employed parents are also more likely than employees without children to forfeit personal time and forgo doing things around the house because of their jobs. Thirty-nine percent of employed parents and 25 percent of employees without children often or very often sacrifice personal time because of their jobs (Figure 4.5). Similarly, 41 percent of employed parents neglect getting things done around the house often or very often, compared with 31 percent of employees without children.

> Thirty-nine percent of employed parents and 25 percent of employees without children often or very often sacrifice personal time because of their jobs.

66 *Personal Well-Being*

Figure 4.5: In the last three months, how often have you not had enough time for yourself because of your job?

Personal Well-Being and Attitudes Toward Employed Mothers

Findings presented in Chapter 3 reveal that a substantial number of employees (41 percent) think it's better if men are the sole breadwinners and women care for the children and home. These findings also indicate that about one-third of employees think that an employed woman cannot have as good a relationship with her children as a woman who is not employed can. In this section, we briefly examine whether discrepancies between such attitudes and employees' actual behavior are related to personal well-being. To focus the analysis, we looked only at employed parents in dual-earner couples for whom the fit between these attitudes and behaviors is most relevant.

When attitudes about employed mothers do not fit the actual behaviors of parents in dual-earner couples, personal well-being suffers in varying degrees.

The exploratory analyses summarized here examine seven measures of personal well-being: stress, coping, burnout, spillover from job to home, general life satisfaction, satisfaction with family life, and satisfaction with marital relationship.

- Employed mothers in dual-earner couples who agree that "It's better for everyone involved if the man earns the money and the woman takes care of the home and children" (50 percent of mothers) have more trouble coping with the demands of daily life and experience more negative spillover from their jobs into their personal lives than employed mothers who disagree with the statement.

- Employed mothers in dual-earner couples who do not agree that "A mother who works outside the home can have just as good a relationship with her children as a mother who does not work" (29 percent of mothers) are more stressed and less satisfied with their lives in general than employed mothers who agree with the statement (71 percent).

- Among employed fathers in dual-earner couples, agreement (44 percent) or disagreement (56 percent) with the statement that "It's better for everyone involved if the man earns the money and the woman takes care of the home and children" has no bearing on personal well-being as represented by the measures examined in this chapter.

- However, employed fathers in dual-earner couples who believe that an employed mother *cannot* have just as good a relationship with her children as a non-employed mother (35.5 percent of fathers) perceive more negative spillover from their jobs into their personal lives and are less satisfied with their lives in general than employed fathers who believe employed mothers can have relationships that are just as good (64.5 percent).

Although these discrepancies between attitudes and behaviors do not have large effects on personal well-being, the findings do suggest a relationship. The extent to which attitudes about employed mothers are rooted in deep-seated cultural values versus firsthand experiences juggling work and family responsibilities, however, remains to be determined.

> Employed mothers in dual-earner couples who agree that "It's better for everyone involved if the man earns the money and the woman takes care of the home and children" have more trouble coping with the demands of daily life and experience more negative spillover from their jobs into their personal lives than employed mothers who disagree with the statement.

68 *Personal Well-Being*

5 Job Characteristics

The characteristics of jobs can have wide-ranging effects on employees' attitudes, feelings, and behavior both at work and in their personal lives. Job characteristics are a special focus of this report because they can be influenced by the actions of employers.

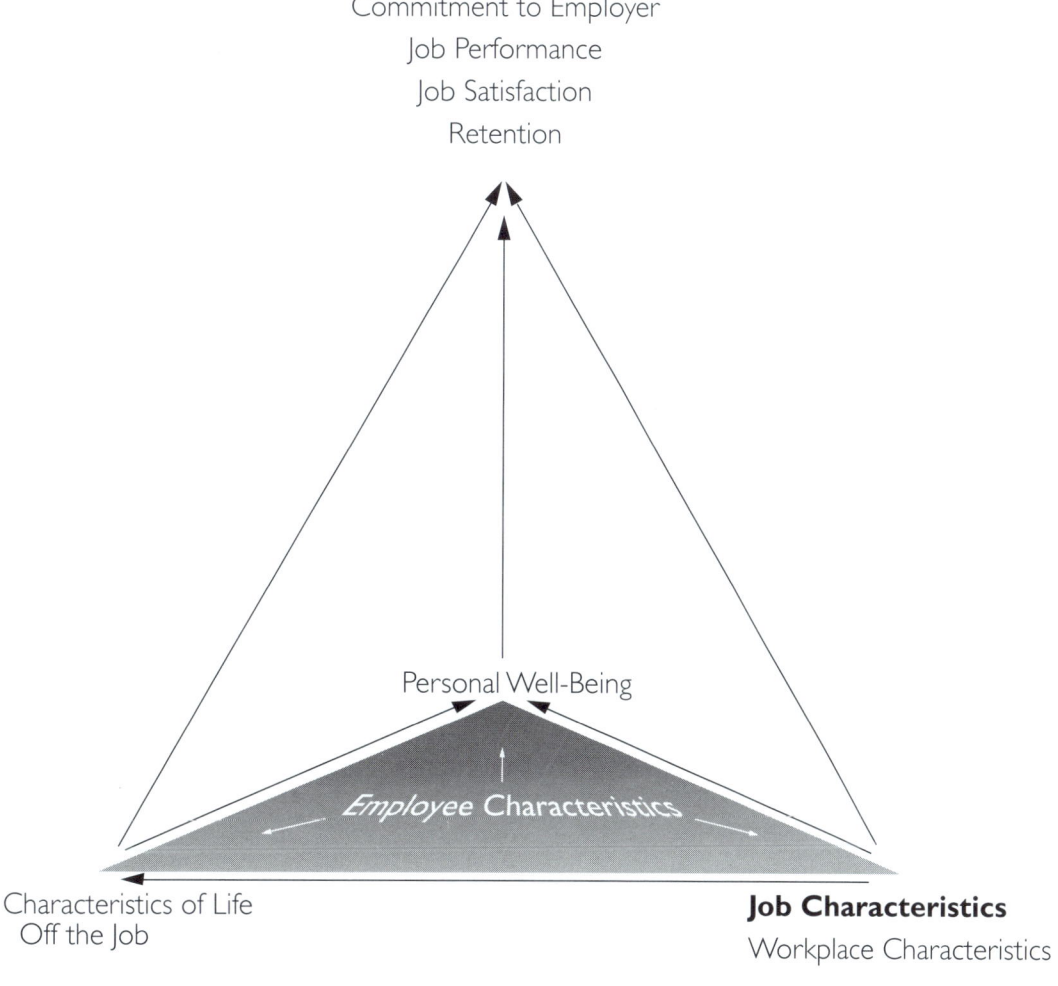

Three dimensions of job characteristics are considered: *job demands*, *job quality*, and *compensation and fringe benefits*. Each of these dimensions is defined by a number of specific interview questions or larger indicators, as described in this chapter. All data refer to employees' main or only jobs.

Job Demands

Job demands include the following primary factors: all paid and unpaid hours worked at main job or only job; number of nights away from home on business during the past three months; frequency of required paid or unpaid overtime with little or no notice; regular daytime shift versus other schedule; frequency of bringing work home; and an index of perceived job pressures that combines responses to several individual questions. Additional data also help to shed light on the demands employees experience on their jobs.

> Seventy-five percent of employed women work regular daytime shifts, compared with 69 percent of men.

Most employees have full-time jobs with regular daytime schedules.

- Eighty-five percent of employees are scheduled to work full-time—35 hours or more a week—at their main or only jobs.

- Seventy-two percent work regular daytime schedules at their main or only jobs, in contrast to 28 percent of employees who work evenings, nights, rotating, split, and variable shifts.

Women are more likely than men to have part-time jobs and are somewhat more likely to work regular daytime shifts.

- Twenty-one percent of employed women are scheduled to work part time—fewer than 35 hours per week—at their main or only jobs, compared with 8 percent of men (Figure 5.1).

> Employees estimate they work, on average, 44.4 paid and unpaid hours per week at their primary jobs.

- Seventy-five percent of employed women work regular daytime shifts, compared with 69 percent of men.

- Among employees working non-daytime schedules, most work full-time (75 percent).

Figure 5.1: Part-Time and Full-Time Employment, Men vs. Women

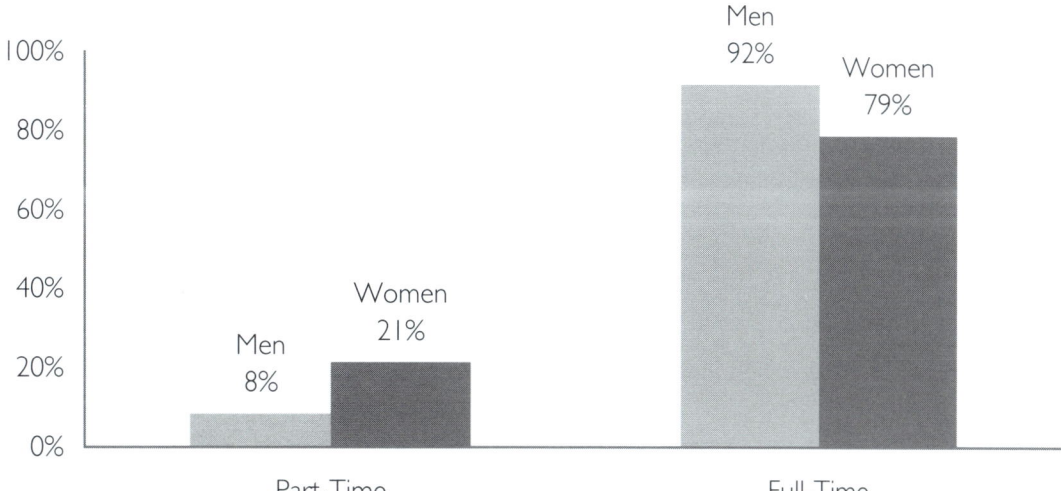

Considering all paid and unpaid hours worked at any location, employees in 1997 spend an average of 44 hours per week on work related to their main or only jobs—six hours more than they are scheduled to work.

The major source of information about work hours in the United States is the U.S. Bureau of Labor Statistics (BLS). However, we discourage comparisons of our findings with those published by the BLS for a number of reasons described in the footnote below.[1] In general, our methodology will produce higher estimates of work hours than those provided by the BLS. This is particularly so when we must restrict 1997 versus 1977 comparisons to employees working 20 or more hours per week.

- Wage and salaried employees estimate they work, on average, 44.4 paid and unpaid hours per week at their primary or only jobs—about six hours more than they are scheduled to work (Table 5.1).

- As reported in Chapter 3, 13 percent of workers have secondary jobs, in addition to their main jobs, at which they work an additional 13 hours per week on average. Including time spent on other jobs, the average hours worked per week increases by 1.6 hours to a total of 46 hours per week.

---

1. Our estimates pertain only to wage and salaried workers 18 and older, whereas BLS estimates generally refer to workers 16 and older and, more often than not, include self-employed workers, as well as unpaid workers in family businesses. It should also be noted that we attempt to estimate usual hours worked, while the BLS estimates hours worked in the last week, which may be substantially reduced by holidays, vacations, time off for illness, slack time, and so forth. We also define total work hours somewhat more broadly than the BLS as all time, paid or unpaid, doing anything related to one's job *at any location*. All of these differences suggest that our estimates are likely to be higher, in general, than those published by the BLS.

Table 5.1: Hours Worked Per Week

Hours Worked	Means *(sample size)*
All Employees:	*(n=2846)*
Scheduled hours at main job	38.5 hrs
Total hours at main job	44.4 hrs
Total hours at all jobs	46.0 hrs
Men:	*(n=1472)*
Scheduled hours at main job	40.7 hrs
Total hours at main job	47.2 hrs
Total hours at all jobs	49.4 hrs
Women:	*(n=1373)*
Scheduled hours at main job	36.3 hrs
Total hours at main job	41.3 hrs
Total hours at all jobs	42.4 hrs
Employed parents with children under 18:	*(n=1308)*
Men's total hours at all jobs	50.9 hrs
Women's total hours at all jobs	41.4 hrs
Employed parents with children under 6:	*(n=534)*
Men's total hours at all jobs	51.6 hrs
Women's total hours at all jobs	40.8 hrs
Married Employees:	*(n=1838)*
Scheduled hours at main job	38.8 hrs
Total hours at main job	44.8 hrs
Total hours at all jobs	46.5 hrs
Single Employees:	*(n=1003)*
Scheduled hours at main job	38.1 hrs
Total hours at main job	43.5 hrs
Total hours at all jobs	45.2 hrs
Employed fathers versus other men:	*(n=1472)*
Fathers' total hours at all jobs	50.9
Other men's total hours at all jobs	48.1
Employed mothers versus other women:	*(n=1373)*
Mother' total hours at all jobs	41.4
Other women's total hours at all jobs	43.3

- On average, men work about seven hours more per week (49.4 hours) than women (42.4 hours) including all paid and unpaid time at all jobs.

- Likewise, employed fathers work more total hours than employed mothers regardless of their children's ages. Among employed parents with children under 18, fathers work nine and one-half more hours per week (50.9 hours) than employed mothers (41.4 hours) at all jobs. Among parents with children under six years old, the gap grows to nearly 11 hours per week, with fathers spending 51.6 hours and mothers 40.8 hours on average at all work related to all jobs.

- There is no significant difference between single and married workers in scheduled hours per week at main jobs or in total hours worked at all jobs; however, singles work about one hour less per week in total (43.5 hours) than married employees (44.8 hours) at their main jobs.

Paid and unpaid work hours at all jobs appear to be longer today than 20 years ago.

- Among employees 18 and older working 20 or more hours per week, all reported paid and unpaid hours at all jobs have risen from 43.6 hours in 1977 to 47.1 hours in 1997, an increase of 3.5 hours per week. While men's total weekly time at all jobs has increased from 47.1 to 49.9 hours—an increase of 2.8 hours per week—women's total hours have increased from 39 to 44 hours—an increase of 5 hours per week.[2]

Given the hours people work, it should come as no surprise that many employees would like to work less.

- As shown in Figure 5.2, 63 percent of employees would like to work fewer hours, considering all paid and unpaid hours at all jobs.

- Men and women are equally likely to prefer fewer work hours, and both would reduce their current time by about 11 hours if they could.

---

2. The slight difference in the percentage of employees wanting to work fewer hours in 1997 as reported here versus Figure 5.2 is due to the fact that workers 65 and older are excluded from the full 1997 in the 1997 versus 1992 comparisons in order to match the 1992 sample.

Figure 5.2: Preferred Work Hours

- Why do employees work longer hours than they prefer? Asked to give their main reason for not working fewer hours, almost half (46 percent) say they need the money, 20 percent say they would not be allowed to reduce their work hours, 16 percent say they work longer hours than they would prefer in order to help their companies succeed, and 5 percent identify themselves as workaholics. The remaining 13 percent of responses are too idiosyncratic to be classified into groups of significant size.

- Women are more likely (51 percent) than men (41 percent) to work more hours than they prefer because they need the money. However, men and women do not differ with respect to the other reasons they give for not working less.

   The proportion of employees—both men and women—who would prefer to work fewer hours per week at their jobs has increased considerably since 1992.

- In 1992, 47 percent of employees said they would prefer to work fewer hours at their jobs. Now, 64 percent want to work fewer hours—an increase of 17 percentage points in 5 years.[2]

- The same trend from 1992 to 1997 holds both for men and women in the labor force.

   Eighteen percent of employees are required to work paid or unpaid overtime hours once a week or more with little or no notice.

- Forty-nine percent of employees estimate they are *required* to work some paid or unpaid overtime with little or no notice at least once a month, and 18 percent do so at least once a

> In 1992, 47 percent of employees said they would prefer to work fewer hours at their jobs. Now, 64 percent want to work fewer hours—an increase of 17 percentage points in 5 years.

week (Table 5.2). Men are more likely than women to work required overtime hours on short notice at least once a month—54 percent of men, compared with 42 percent of women.

Although "required" overtime with little or no notice is unlikely to account for the six-hour weekly difference between scheduled and total hours worked on main jobs (Table 5.1), total work hours do also include voluntary paid and unpaid extra hours worked at any location.

One in five employees has taken an overnight business trip in the past three months.

- Twelve percent of employees spent between one and five nights away from home on business travel during the past three months, while 9 percent spent six or more nights on the road. Employed men are almost twice as likely (27 percent) as women (15 percent) to travel overnight on business at least once every three months.

Table 5.2: Overtime, Taking Work Home, and Business Travel

Job Demands	Percentage (sample size)
Overtime with No Notice:	(n=2877)
Never	20%
Less than once a month	32
About once a month	31
Once a week	18
Frequency of Bringing Work Home:	(n=2877)
Never	49%
Once a month or less	20
Once a week	15
More than once a week	16
Nights Away from Home on Business over Past Three Months:	(n=2854)
None in past 3 months	79%
1 through 5 nights in past 3 months	12
6 or more nights in past 3 months	9
Average nights away from home	2 nights

- The average number of nights away from home on business in the past three months for the entire sample is two, with men traveling overnight more often (three nights) than women (one night).

Nearly one-third of employees bring work home once or more often per week.

- Almost one-third of employees (31 percent) spend time on a weekly basis doing work at home that is directly related to their main jobs. Employed men and women are equally likely to bring work home.

Employees today are more likely to bring work home from the job than employees 20 years ago were.

- The proportion of employees bringing work home from the job once a week or more has increased by 10 percentage points since 1977, while the proportion never bringing work home from the job has decreased by 16 percentage points. This change may have been abetted by a shift *toward* new technologies and *away* from jobs that can be performed only at the worksite.

> Forty-nine percent of employees estimate they are *required* to work some paid or unpaid overtime with little or no notice at least once a month, and 18 percent are required do so at least once a week.

Job pressures have increased substantially over the past 20 years.

The three items considered here are averaged to produce a single index of *job pressure* for purposes of analysis in Chapter 8.

- Sixty-eight percent of workers agree with the statement: "My job requires that I work very fast"—a 13 percentage point increase since 1977, when 55 percent of workers agreed (Figure 5.3).[3]

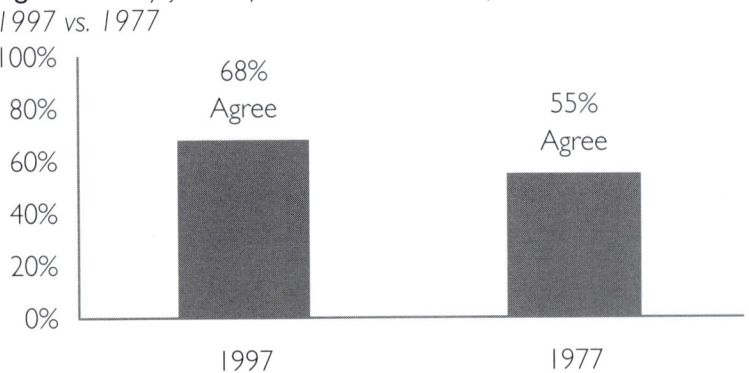

Figure 5.3: My job requires that I work very fast.
1997 vs. 1977

- Today, 88 percent of employees agree with the statement: "My job requires that I work very hard"—up from 70 percent in 1977 (Figure 5.4).

---

3. For purposes of comparison, the 1997 sample was reduced to employees working 20 or more hours per week and interviewed in English, while the 1977 sample was reduced to employees 18 and older.

Figure 5.4: My job requires that I work very hard.
1997 vs. 1977

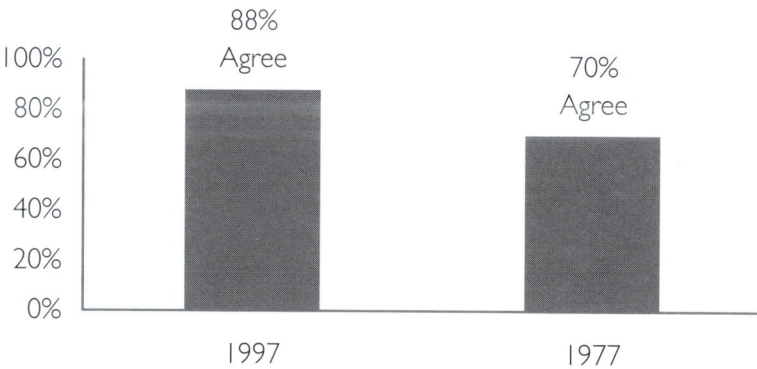

- The biggest change in employees' perceptions of job pressures relates to time. In 1997, 60 percent of workers agree with the statement: "I never seem to have enough time to get everything done on my job"—a dramatic increase from 40 percent in 1977 (Figure 5.5).

Figure 5.5: Never Enough Time to Get Everything Done on Job
1997 vs. 1977

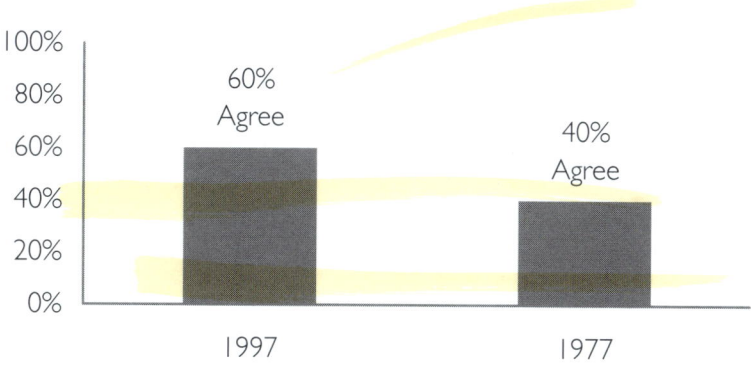

Job Quality

Job quality includes five factors: job autonomy, learning opportunities on the job, meaningfulness of job, opportunities for advancement on the job, and job security.

Most employees feel they have some measure of autonomy in their jobs.

The three items examined here are averaged to produce a single index of *job autonomy* for analyses in Chapter 8.

- Nearly three-quarters of employees agree that they can decide what they do on their jobs (Table 5.3).

- More than four in five employees (85 percent) feel that it is essentially their responsibility to decide how their jobs get done.

- Seventy-percent of employees have a lot of say in what happens on their jobs.

Employees in 1997 have significantly more job autonomy than employees did 20 years ago.[4]

- Job autonomy has increased significantly over the past 20 years. Compared with workers in 1977, today's employees have more freedom to decide what they do on their jobs (74 percent versus 56 percent), more responsibility in deciding how their jobs get done (86 percent versus 80 percent), and more say in what happens on their jobs (71 percent versus 59 percent).

> Compared with workers in 1977, today's employees have more freedom to decide what they do on their jobs (74 percent versus 56 percent), more responsibility in deciding how their jobs get done (86 percent versus 80 percent), and more say in what happens on their jobs (71 percent versus 59 percent).

---

4. For purposes of comparison, the 1997 sample was reduced to employees working 20 or more hours per week and interviewed in English, while the 1977 sample was reduced to employees 18 and older.

Table 5.3: Employees' Perceptions of Job Autonomy

Job Autonomy Items	Full 1997 Sample	1997 vs. 1977 Restricted Samples for Comparisons [a]		
		NSCW 1997	*Sig.*	QES 1977
	Percentage (sample size)	Percentage (sample size)		Percentage (sample size)
I have the freedom to decide what I do on my job.	(n=2757)	(n=2707)	***	(n=1265)
Disagree	26%	26%		44%
Agree	74	74		56
It is basically my own responsibility to decide how my job gets done.	(n=2769)	(n=2721)	**	(n=1274)
Disagree	15%	14%		20%
Agree	85	86		80
I have a lot of say about what happens on my job.	(n=2762)	(n=2714)	***	(n=1269)
Disagree	30%	29%		41%
Agree	70	71		59

[a] For purposes of comparison, the 1997 sample was reduced to employees working 20 or more hours per week and interviewed in English, while the 1977 sample was reduced to employees 18 and older. Percentages differ slightly for the full and restricted 1997 samples.

Significance levels: * = $p < .01$; ** = $p < .001$; *** = $p < .0001$; ns = not significant.

Most employees have jobs that provide learning opportunities.

The four items examined here are averaged to provide a single index of *learning opportunities* for analysis in Chapter 8.

- Nine in 10 workers (90 percent) agree with the statement: "My job requires that I keep learning new things." (Table 5.4) Employees in management and professional positions are more likely (96 percent) than workers in other occupational groups (86 percent) to be challenged to learn new things on the job.

- Three in four employees (76 percent) agree that their jobs require creativity. Employees in management and professional jobs have much more opportunity for creativity (91 percent) than workers in other occupational groups (69 percent). Also, men are somewhat more likely to work in jobs that require creativity than women—79 percent versus 74 percent.

- Ninety-two percent of employees agree with the statement: "My job lets me use my skills and abilities." Employees in professional and management positions are more able to use their knowledge and skills in their current jobs (96 percent) than employees in other occupational groups (89 percent).

- About three in four workers (78 percent) are generally satisfied with the opportunities they have at work to learn new skills that could help them get better jobs or find other equally good jobs if their current jobs do not work out.

Over the past 20 years, opportunities and challenges to learn on the job have increased substantially.

- As shown in Table 5.4, the proportion of employees with jobs that require them to keep learning new things has increased by eight percentage points since 1977, while the proportion with jobs that require them to be creative has increased by 17 percentage points. Employees in 1997 are also more likely to feel that their jobs allow them to use their own skills and abilities—an increase of 16 percentage points from 1977.

Table 5.4: Learning Opportunities on the Job

Learning Opportunities	Full 1997 Sample	1997 vs. 1977 Restricted Samples for Comparisons[a]		
		NSCW 1997	Sig.	QES 1977
	Percentage (sample size)	Percentage (sample size)		Percentage (sample size)
My job requires that I keep learning new things.	(n=2869)	(n=2718)	***	(n=1268)
Disagree	10%	10%		18%
Agree	90	90		82
My job requires that I be creative.	(n=2867)	(n=2716)	***	(n=1275)
Disagree	24%	24%		41%
Agree	76	76		59
My job lets me use my skills and abilities.	(n=2868)	(n=2718)	***	(n=1272)
Disagree	8%	8%		23.5%
Agree	92	92		76.5
How satisfied are you with the opportunities that you have at work to learn new skills that could help you get a better job or find another equally good job if this one does not work out?	(n=2841)	Not asked in 1977		
Not satisfied	22%			
Satisfied	78			

[a] For purposes of comparison, the 1997 sample was reduced to employees working 20 or more hours per week and interviewed in English, while the 1977 sample was reduced to employees 18 and older. Percentages differ slightly for the full and restricted 1997 samples.

Significance levels: * = p < .01; ** = p < .001; *** = p < .0001; ns = not significant.

In general, jobs full of learning opportunities appear to be a good thing for employees and employers.

- Supplemental analyses[5] reveal that employees with more learning opportunities and challenges on the job have more positive feelings toward their jobs and employers.

- Employees whose jobs let them use their skills and abilities and who are satisfied with the learning opportunities available on the job report greater personal well-being—lower levels of stress, more effective coping, less job burnout, and less negative spillover from work into personal life. Employees whose jobs require creativity report lower levels of job burnout but otherwise exhibit the same levels of personal well-being as other employees. The only finding that suggests a possible negative effect is that employees who are *required* to keep learning new things on the job are slightly more likely to experience spillover from their jobs into their personal lives.

Unfortunately, we did not ask questions that directly identify employees who want fewer challenges and learning opportunities. It may be that for these employees, having to keep learning new things and solving new problems on the job is an unwanted demand with negative consequences on and off the job.

Most employees find the work they do meaningful, and the proportion who feel this way has increased over the past 20 years.

- Ninety percent of employees agreed with the statement: "The work I do on my job is meaningful to me." (Figure 5.6) Our analyses reveal that employees in management and professional jobs are more likely (96 percent) than employees in other occupational groups (87 percent) to find the work they do on their main jobs meaningful.

- Comparing 1997 with 1977,[6] we find an increase of seven percentage points in the proportions of employees who find their work meaningful to them.

> Employees whose jobs let them use their skills and abilities and who are satisfied with the learning opportunities available on the job report greater personal well-being—lower levels of stress, more effective coping, less job burnout, and less negative spillover from work into their personal lives.

---

5. These analyses relied upon simple bivariate correlations among the variables cited.

6. For purposes of comparison, the 1997 sample was reduced to employees working 20 or more hours per week and interviewed in English, while the 1977 sample was reduced to employees 18 and older. Percentages differ slightly for the full and restricted 1997 samples.

Figure 5.6: The work I do on my job is meaningful to me.

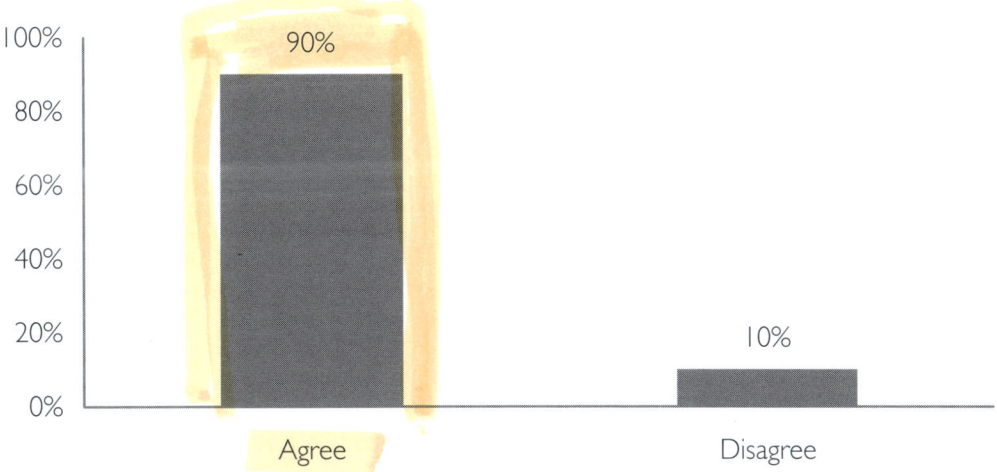

Only 16 percent of workers rate their chances for advancement in their jobs as excellent.

- Sixteen percent of employees rate their own chances to advance in their organizations as excellent, while an additional 23 percent would rate their chances as good (Figure 5.7). In stark contrast, 61 percent—three in five workers—rate their chances for advancement as poor or only fair.

Figure 5.7: How would you rate your own chance to advance in your organization?

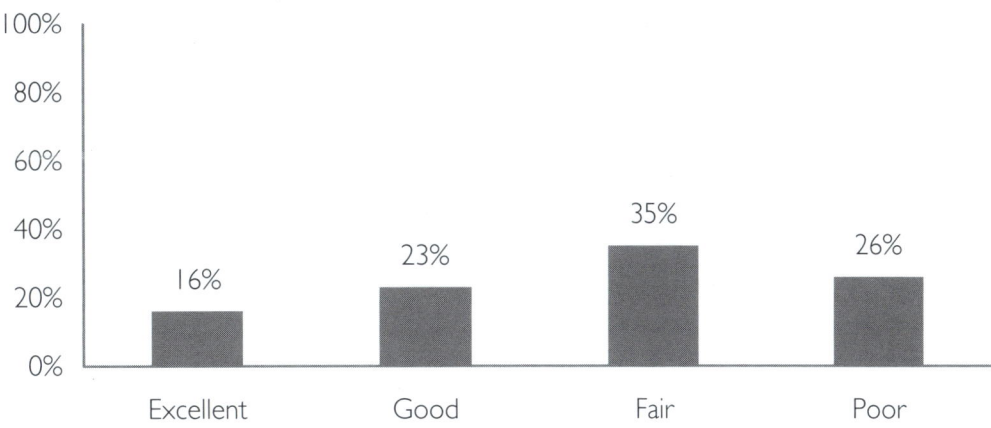

About three out of 10 employees think it is somewhat or very likely they will lose their jobs in the next couple of years. Job security has decreased over the past 20 years.

- Thirty percent of employees think it is somewhat or very likely that during the next couple of years they will lose their current jobs and have to look for one with another employer (Figure 5.8). Men are just as likely as women (30 percent) to think they might lose their jobs over the next few years. This sense of job insecurity cuts across occupational groups; there is no difference between employees in professional and management jobs and employees in other occupational categories.

> In 1977, only 15 percent of employees thought it was likely they would lose their jobs in the next couple of years—14 percentage points lower than today's 29 percent of employees who feel insecure in their jobs.

- In 1977, only 15 percent of employees thought it was likely they would lose their jobs in the next couple of years and have to find a new one with another employer—14 percentage points lower than today's 29 percent of employees who feel insecure in their jobs. Forty-five percent of employees in 1977, versus 30 percent today, thought it was not at all likely they would lose their jobs.

Figure 5.8: How Likely to Lose Current Job in Next Couple of Years

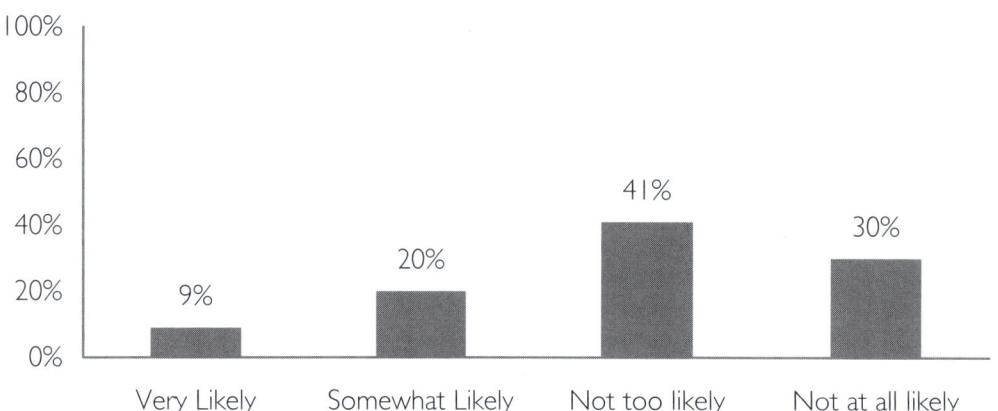

About one-third of employees think it would be very difficult to find a job with another employer that provides approximately the same income and fringe benefits as their current jobs.

- Thirty-nine percent of employees feel that it would be "not at all easy" to find a job with another employer that would provide approximately the same income and fringe benefits they have now, while 61 percent feel it would be somewhat or very easy to do so (Figure 5.9).

Figure 5.9: How Easy to Find Another Job with Comparable Pay and Benefits

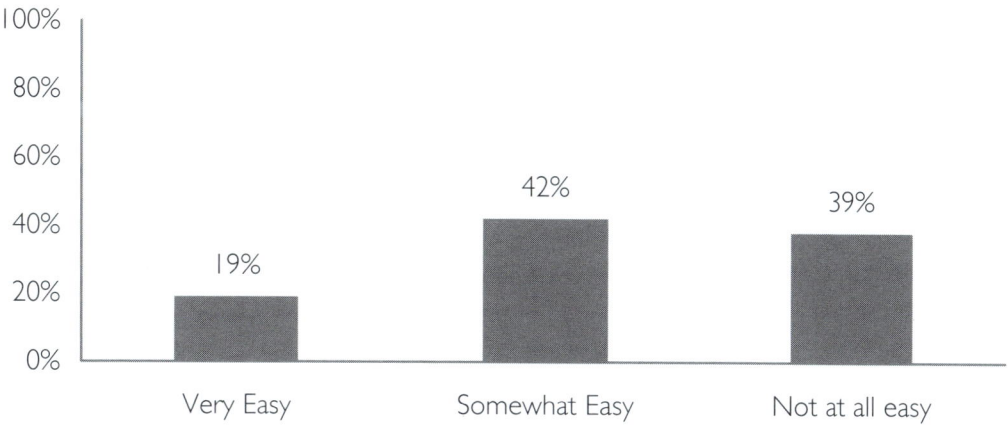

Among employees who think it is somewhat or very likely they may lose their jobs over the next couple of years, 45 percent think it would be very difficult to find another job with comparable pay and benefits.

- Forty-five percent of employees who think they are somewhat or very likely to lose their jobs within the next two years think it will be "not at all easy" to find a job with another employer offering approximately the same pay and fringe benefits as they have now. Forty percent think it will be somewhat easy to find a job comparable to the one they have now, and 15 percent think it will be very easy.

Compensation and Fringe Benefits

Wage and salaried workers report median current hourly earnings of $12 at their primary jobs and median estimated annual earnings of $30,000 from all jobs.

- Both mean and median earnings are shown in Table 5.5. Mean earnings are substantially higher than median earnings because the federal minimum wage establishes a lower threshold, while there is no cap at the higher end of the earnings continuum. Comparable earnings estimates are not available for 1977.

Among all employees 18 and older in the wage and salaried labor force, the average earnings of men are substantially higher than the average earnings of women.

Although there are various factors that account for at least part of the earnings difference between men and women, we do not address this issue here.

- Men earn an average of $21.38 per hour at their primary jobs, while women earn an average of $15.05—a difference of $6.33 per hour. The difference in median hourly earnings is much smaller, with men having median hourly earnings of $13.98 and women earning a median of $10.22 per hour—a difference of $3.76 per hour.

- Men estimated that that their total earnings for all of 1997 from all jobs would be $43,754 on average, much higher than women's estimate of $28,060—a difference of $15,694. The difference in median projected annual earnings for men and women is also large—$12,000—though smaller than for average projected annual earnings.

Table 5.5: Compensation

Hourly and Annual Earnings	Mean and Median *(sample size)*
Hourly Earnings Before Taxes and Other Deductions at Main Job:	
All Employees	*(n=2597)*
Mean (average)	$18.36
Median[a]	$12.00
Men	*(n=1357)*
Mean (average)	$21.38
Median[a]	$13.98
Women	*(n=1240)*
Mean (average)	$15.05
Median[a]	$10.22
Estimated Annual Earnings from All Jobs for All of 1997 Before Taxes and Other Deductions:	
All Employees	*(n=2556)*
Mean (average)	$36,372
Median[a]	$30,000
Men	*(n=1354)*
Mean (average)	$43,754
Median[a]	$36,000
Women	*(n=1202)*
Mean (average)	$28,060
Median[a]	$24,000

[a] *Fifty percent of employees have earnings below the median; 50 percent above.*

Traditional Fringe Benefits

Traditional fringe benefits include access to health insurance for the employee and the employee's family, employer contributions to health insurance plans, pension or retirement plans, employer contributions to retirement plans, paid vacation days, paid holidays, and time off for personal illness without loss of pay. All of these benefits are cash-like in that employers can calculate their monetary costs and employees can assess their monetary value. Although we did not attempt to collect detailed information from employees about all possible benefit packages, we believe that together the general measures of access examined here provide an accurate assessment of the overall generosity of traditional benefits on the job. The number of individual benefits offered were totaled to produce a single index of access to *traditional fringe benefits* for purposes of analysis in Chapter 8. Comparisons are not made with 1977 because the questions differed, and only two comparisons could be made with 1992.

More than four out of five workers have access to personal health insurance coverage through their jobs, and nine out of 10 are covered from some source.

- Eighty-four percent of all employees have access to personal health insurance coverage through their main jobs (Table 5.6), and most of those (84 percent) currently use the personal coverage offered through their employers. Access to personal health insurance coverage has not changed since 1992.

- Ninety-one percent of employees are covered from some source—spouse, partner, Medicaid, Medicare, private plan—leaving only nine percent without any health insurance coverage.

Part-time and low-wage employees are much less likely than other employees to have access to health insurance benefits through their jobs.

- Employees who work part-time at their main jobs—fewer than 35 scheduled hours per week—are much less likely (51 percent) than full-time employees (90 percent) to have access to personal health insurance coverage, and the proportion with access continues to decline as work hours decrease. However, 84 percent of part-time employees have coverage from some source.

- Low-wage employees—the bottom quartile of wage earners—are also much less likely (65 percent) than other workers (90 percent) to have access to personal health coverage, and 18 percent do not have coverage from any source.

> Employees who work part-time at their main jobs—fewer than 35 scheduled hours per week—are much less likely than full-time employees to have access to personal health insurance coverage, and the proportion with access continues to decline as work hours decrease.

About one-quarter of employees have access to personal health insurance plans that are fully paid for by their employers, and about half have plans that are partially paid for by their employers.

- While 16 percent of employees have no access to health insurance on the job and 4 percent have to cover all the insurance costs to participate, 53 percent have plans that are partially paid for by their employers and 27 percent have plans fully paid for by their employers.

Access to family health insurance coverage through the job parallels access to personal coverage, with about four in five employees having access to family plans.

- Eighty-one percent of employees are offered health insurance for family members (Table 5.6), and 86 percent of these employees participate in the plans offered. Access to family coverage has not changed since 1992.

- However, 94 percent of employees have health insurance coverage for their children from some private or public source. This still leaves 6 percent without any coverage for their children.

Part-time and low-wage employees are much less likely than other employees to have access to family coverage.

- Only 45 percent of part-time employees working fewer than 35 scheduled hours per week at their main jobs have access to family health insurance benefits, compared with 87 percent of full-time employees—a difference of 42 percentage points. In addition, substantially, fewer low-wage employees are offered family health insurance benefits (59 percent) than other workers (88 percent).

- Although 92 percent of part-time employees and 89 percent of low-wage employees have coverage for their children from some source, this still leaves eight percent of children of part-time workers and 11 percent of children of low-wage workers without any health insurance coverage.

Health insurance costs shift somewhat from employers to employees when it comes to family coverage.

- Only 17 percent of employees have employers who pick up the complete tab for family health insurance coverage, while 27 percent can participate in personal health insurance plans at no charge (Table 5.6). Ten percent have to pay the entire cost of family coverage, which represents substantial monthly payments.

Three-quarters of employees have pension or retirement plans at work, and two-thirds have plans to which their employers make contributions.

- Seventy-five percent of employees have access to pension or retirement plans on their jobs, and 66 percent of all employees have employers who contribute to pension or retirement plans at work (Table 5.6).

- Among employees with retirement plans, 71 percent report making personal contributions of some amount.

Most employees receive some paid vacation time, paid holidays, and paid time off for personal illness. However, part-time, hourly, and low-wage employees are less likely than other workers to have these benefits.

- Eighty-two percent of all employees receive some amount of paid vacation time, 81 percent have some paid holidays, and 74 percent have some time off for personal illness (Table 5.6).

Table 5.6: Traditional Fringe Benefits at Primary Job

Traditional Benefits	Percentage (sample size)
Is personal health insurance available through your main job?	(n=2864)
Yes	84%
No	16
Is personal health insurance coverage paid by your employer?	(n=2864)
Yes, entirely	27%
Yes, partly	53
No, employees pay	4
Not available	16
Is health insurance coverage for family members available to you through your job?	(n=2864)
Yes	81%
No	19
Is the cost of insurance for family members paid by your employer?	(n=2864)
Yes, entirely	17%
Yes, partly	53
No, employees pay	10
Not available	19
Is any kind of pension or retirement plan available to you through your job?	(n=2847)
Yes	75%
No	25
Has retirement plan to which employer contributes:	(n=2054)
Yes	66%
No	34
Do you receive paid vacation days?	(n=2871)
Yes	82%
No	18
Do you receive any paid holidays?	(n=2870)
Yes	80.5%
No	19.5
Are you allowed some paid time off for personal illness?	(n=2849)
Yes	74%
No	26

- Only 48 percent of part-time employees, versus 88 percent of full-time employees, receive any paid vacation days—a difference of 40 percentage points (Figure 5.10). Hourly employees are somewhat less likely (80 percent) than salaried workers (85 percent) to have paid vacation time. Low-wage employees are substantially less likely (66 percent) than other workers (86 percent) to have paid vacation time—a difference of 20 percentage points.

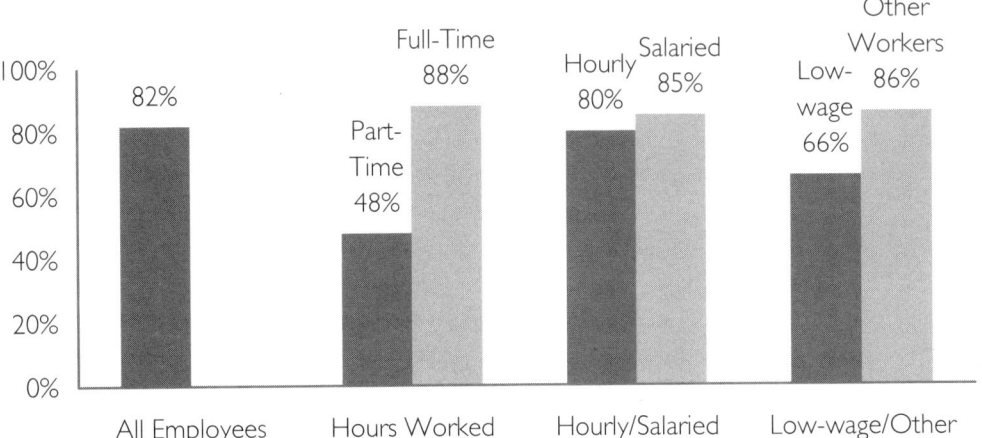

Figure 5.10: Percentage with Paid Vacation Time at Primary Job

- Only 50 percent of part-time employees, versus 86 percent of full-time employees, receive paid holidays—a difference of 36 percentage points (Figure 5.11). Hourly workers are also somewhat less likely than salaried workers to have paid holidays—78 versus 86 percent. As well, low-wage employees are less likely (65 percent) than other workers (86 percent) to have paid holidays—a difference of 21 percentage points.

Figure 5.11: Percentage with Paid Holidays at Primary Job

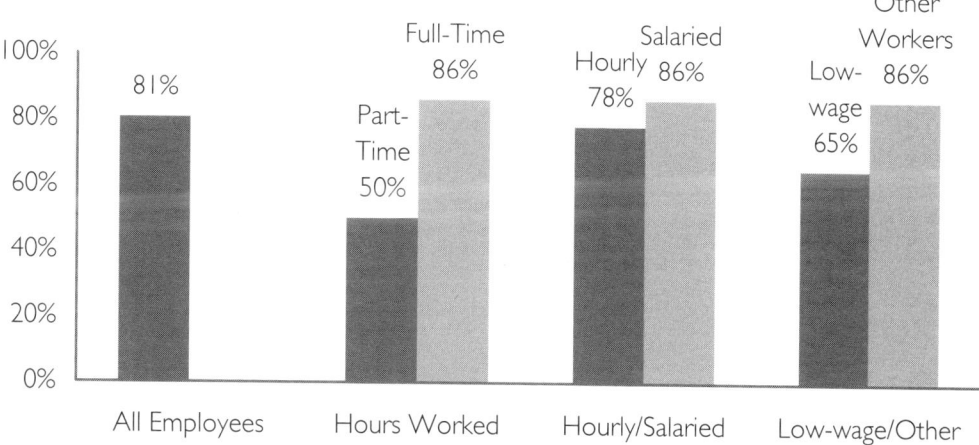

- Only 50 percent of part-time workers, versus 78 percent of full-time workers, receive paid time off for personal illness—a difference of 28 percentage points (Figure 5.12). Hourly workers are also less likely (66 percent) than salaried workers (87 percent) to receive paid sick time—a difference of 21 percentage points. And only, 58 percent of low-wage employees receive paid sick time compared with 79 percent for other workers—a difference of 21 percentage points.

Figure 5.12: Percentage with Paid Personal Sick Time at Primary Job

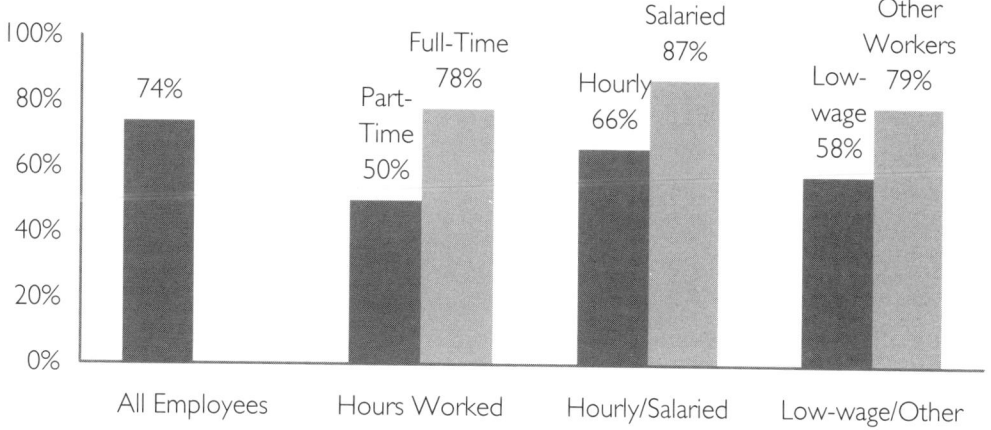

Employees who work for larger companies have access to more traditional fringe benefits than those who work for smaller companies.

- Using our index of traditional fringe benefit availability, large companies (1,000 or more employees nationally) provide more benefits that medium-size companies (50 through 99 employees nationally) and small companies (fewer than 50 employees nationally). Medium-size companies also offer more benefits than small companies.

Dependent-Care Benefits

Dependent-care benefits include five components: child care resource and referral services, child care services operated or sponsored by the employer, direct financial assistance for purchasing child care services, dependent-care assistance plans to which employees can contribute pretax income for the purchase of child and dependent-elder care services, and elder care resource and referral, which apply both to dependent and non-dependent elders. As with traditional fringe benefits, these benefits have a cash-like quality, at least for employers who account for service contracts as well as internal program costs. We did not attempt to collect exhaustive information about all possible dependent-care benefits from employees. We counted the benefits offered to produce a single index of *dependent-care benefits* available on the job for analyses that will be conducted in Chapter 8.

Dependent-care benefits are much less widely available than traditional fringe benefits.

- As shown in Table 5.7, relatively few employees have access to dependent-care benefits through their jobs: 20 percent have access to services intended to help them find child care arrangements for their children, 11 percent work for employers who operate or sponsor a child care program at or near the workplace, 13 percent have employers who provide some form of financial assistance to help pay for child care, and 29 percent are able to have pretax deductions made from their paychecks to be used to purchase care for children or dependent elders.

> Twenty percent of employees have access to services intended to help them find child care arrangements for their children.

Because employees without dependent care responsibilities may not even be aware that these benefits are offered, it is likely that their availability is somewhat underreported, as is suggested by the large number of "don't know" responses noted in Table 5.7.

Although no comparisons with 1977 were possible, we did compare the availability of child care information and referral services, on- or near-site child care centers, and elder care information and referral services for 1992 and 1997. Only access to elder care information and referral services changed, increasing from 11 percent in 1992 to 25 percent in 1997.

Employees with children under 13 and under six years old have the same limited access to child care benefits as other workers.

- The proportions of employees with and without children who report having access to child care benefits are the same.

Employees who have provided care for elders in the past year report having somewhat greater access than other workers to elder care information and referral services.

- Thirty-one percent of employees who have provided elder care in the past year, compared with 23 percent who have not had elder care responsibilities, report that their employers provide assistance in obtaining elder care information and services. This difference in reported access may simply result from differences in knowledge about the availability of elder care services.

Employees who work for larger companies have access to more dependent-care benefits than those who work for smaller companies.

- Using our index of dependent-care benefits availability, large companies (1,000 or more employees nationally) provide more benefits that medium-size companies (50 through 99 employees nationally) and small companies (fewer than 50 employees nationally). Medium-size companies also offer more benefits than small companies.

- In our 1992 study we also found that larger companies were more likely to provide traditional and dependent-care benefits, which may impose substantial direct costs on employers. However, smaller companies and smaller worksites came into their own when we examined flexible work arrangements, which will be considered in the next chapter of this report.

Table 5.7: Dependent-care Benefits

Dependent-care Benefits	Percentage *(sample size)*
Does your employer have a program or service that helps employees find child care?	*(n=2655)*
Yes	20%
No	80
[Don't know: n = 222]	
Does your employer operate or sponsor a child care center for employees' children on or near the worksite?	*(n=2807)*
Yes	11%
No	89
[Don't know: n = 70]	
Does your employer provide employees with any direct financial assistance for child care?	*(n=2756)*
Yes	13%
No	87
[Don't know: n = 121]	
Does your employer have a program that allows employees to put part of their pay—before taxes—into an account that can be used to pay for child care or other dependent care?	*(n=2670)*
Yes	29%
No	71
[Don't know: n = 207]	
Does your employer have a program that helps employees get information about elder care or find services for elderly relatives?	*(n=2626)*
Yes	25%
No	75
[Don't know: n = 250]	

6 Workplace Characteristics

Like job characteristics, the characteristics of workplaces can affect employees' attitudes, feelings, and behavior both on and off the job. Workplace culture and social climate are affected by the actions of employers, though until recently, most employers have not viewed these factors as pivotal in meeting bottom-line business objectives. Along with job characteristics, workplace characteristics provide the foundation for the business leg of our conceptual model.

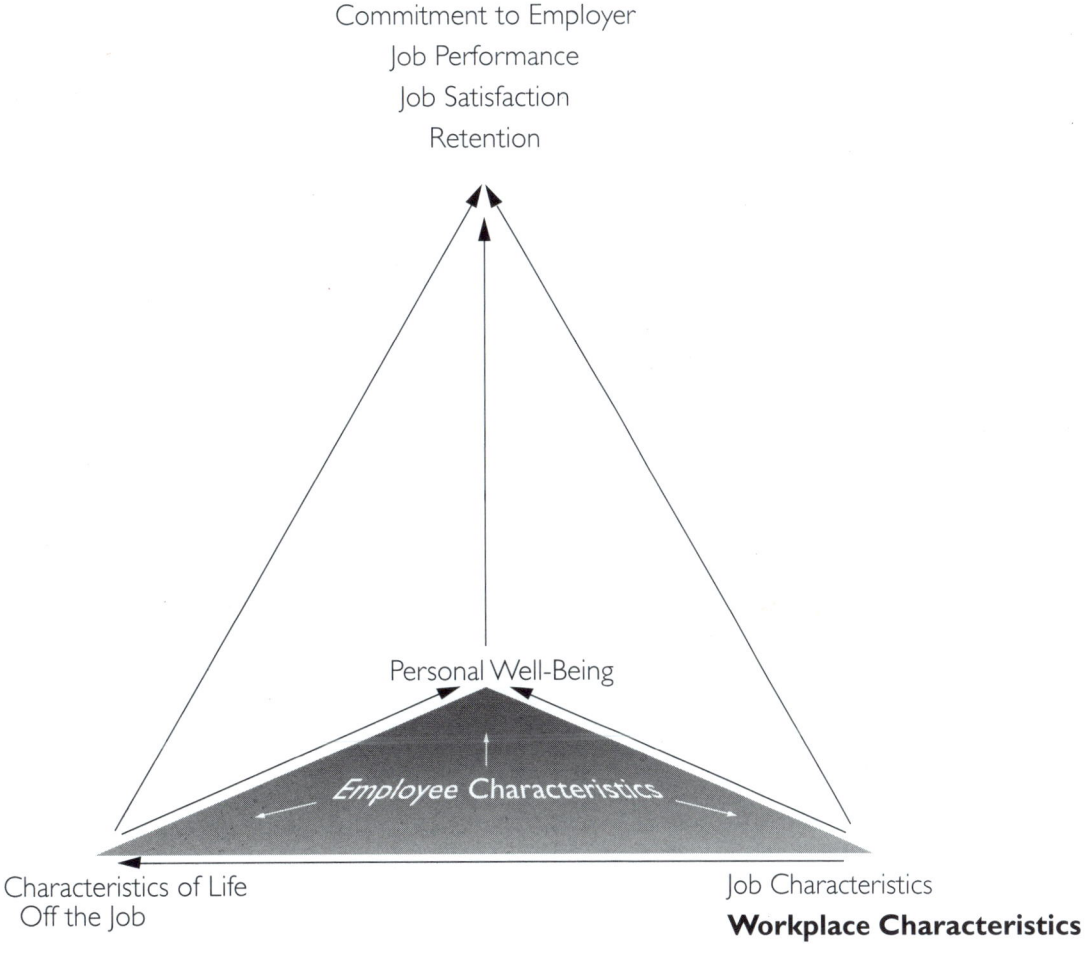

Twenty-nine questions are used to measure workplace characteristics. Most are combined into five more general indicators—*flexible work arrangements, supervisor support, supportiveness of workplace culture, coworker relations,* and *discrimination*—for later analyses. Two questions stand alone as indicators of *equal opportunity* and *respect* on the job. We compare, where possible, data from 1997 with data from the 1992 National Study of the Changing Workforce (NSCW) and 1977 Quality of Employment Survey (QES). Only the questions related to discrimination were asked in the 1977 QES; however, most of the other items were included in the 1992 NSCW.

Flexible Work Arrangements

Although some of the flexible arrangements described in Table 6.1 are treated as fringe benefits by individual employers, here we view them as aspects of the workplace environment. The questions asked in the 1997 survey were not designed to determine whether these flexible arrangements are formal policies affecting all workers, normative practices in the workplace, or case-by-case decisions made by supervisors. Moreover, these arrangements, unlike traditional fringe benefits and dependent-care benefits, cannot be readily translated into direct costs to employers or monetary value for employees. Responses to all of the questions listed in Table 6.1 were combined to produce an overall index of *flexibility* for the analyses conducted in Chapter 8.

Nearly half of all employees are able to choose—within some range of hours—when they begin and end their workdays, but only one in four can change daily schedules as needed.

- Forty-five percent of employees are allowed to choose—within a range of hours—their own starting and quitting times, what we refer to as *traditional flextime* (Figure 6.1).

- Far fewer employees (25 percent) are allowed to change their starting and quitting times on a daily basis as needed.

Figure 6.1: Flextime at Work

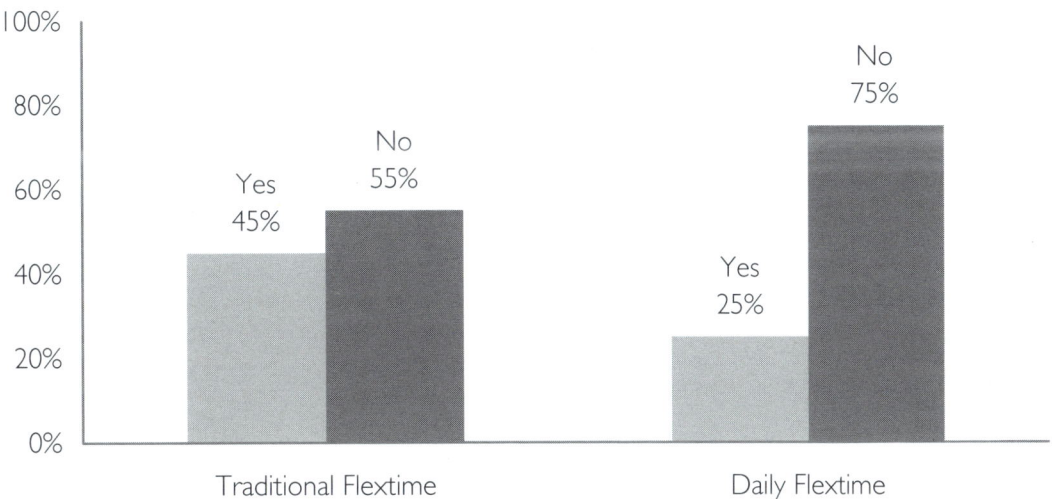

Two-thirds of employees find it relatively easy to take time off during the workday to address family or personal matters.

- Although only 25 percent of employees (Figure 6.1) are allowed to make daily changes in their work schedules to meet personal needs, 66 percent find it "not too hard" or "not hard at all" to take time off during the workday to deal with family or personal matters (Table 6.1). Our analyses reveal no differences between men and women.

Only one-half of employed parents are able to take a few days off from work to care for sick children without losing pay, forfeiting vacation time, or having to fabricate some excuse for missing work.

- Only 50 percent of employed parents with children under 18 are allowed to take a few days off to care for sick children without losing pay, forfeiting vacation days, or having to make up some excuse for their absences. This proportion is the same for men and women (Table 6.1).

- Employed parents in management and professional jobs, however, are more likely (62 percent) than employed parents in other occupations (43 percent) to be allowed to take time off from work to care for a sick child without losing pay, forfeiting vacation time, or having to make up an excuse for their absences.

Employed fathers in dual-earner couples who are allowed to take a few days off to care for sick children—without losing pay, forfeiting vacation time, or having to fabricate some excuse for missing work—are more likely than fathers without this option to attend to children's needs.

- Findings reported in Chapter 3 (Figure 3.17) reveal that employed fathers in dual-earner couples are much less likely (22 percent) than employed mothers in dual-earner couples (83 percent) to be the ones most likely to take time off work to *attend to their children's needs* when both parents are supposed to be at their jobs. However, fathers who are allowed time off to care for sick children—without losing pay, forfeiting vacation days, or having to make up some excuse for their absences—are more likely (29 percent) than other fathers (17 percent) to take time off work to attend to children's needs when both parents are supposed to be at their jobs.

Although children's special needs during work hours include more than receiving care when they are sick, ensuring care for a sick child is arguably one of the most urgent needs employed parents face on a regular basis. As our findings suggest, workplaces that make it financially feasible and legitimate for both male and female employees to address such needs may encourage fathers to assume greater parental responsibilities than they would otherwise.

Nearly all employees in companies of all sizes say that women are able to take time off—without jeopardizing their jobs—to recuperate from childbirth, and most say that men can take time off when they become fathers.

The Family and Medical Leave Act (FMLA), passed by Congress and signed into law in 1993, provides all employees working in companies with 50 or more employees 12 weeks of unpaid, job-guaranteed leave for the birth, adoption, or foster placement of a child. The 1997 sample includes employees working for employers both covered under and exempt from this federal statute.

- Ninety-four percent of employees indicate that women at their places of employment are able to take an unspecified amount of time off work, without endangering their jobs, to recuperate from childbirth (Table 6.1). The same proportion is reported by men and women, by managers/professionals and employees in other occupations, and by employees whose local employers are covered by (50 or more employees) and exempt (fewer than 50 employees) from FMLA requirements.

- A smaller proportion of employees (80 percent) indicate that men at their places of employment are able to take an unspecified amount of time off work, without endangering their jobs, when they become fathers. The same proportion is reported by men and women and by employees whose local employers are covered by (50 or more employees) and exempt (fewer than 50 employees) from FMLA requirements. However, fewer employees in non-management and non-professional jobs (78 percent) than managers and professionals (83 percent) say that men who work for their same employers are able to take some time off, without jeopardizing their jobs, when they become fathers.

> Fewer employees in non-management and non-professional jobs than managers and professionals say that men at their workplace are able to take some time off, without jeopardizing their jobs, when they become fathers.

Part-time employees feel they have more opportunities to switch to full-time in their current jobs than full-time workers have to work part-time.

- When part-timers were asked whether they could arrange to work full-time in their current positions, 58 percent said yes or maybe. In contrast, when full-timers were asked whether they could work part-time in their current positions, 38 percent said yes or maybe—a difference of 20 percentage points (Table 6.1).

Movement to and from full-time and part-time status *with the same employer and in the same job* has not received much attention in discussions of workplace flexibility. However, changes in hours worked—whether or not for the same employer and in the same job—are related, for many workers, to such life-cycle changes as students working part-time while classes are in session and full-time during breaks, then taking full-time, full-year positions upon graduation; women working full-time when they first enter the labor force, part-time when their children are very young, and full-time again when their children are older; and retirees downshifting to part-time during their last few years of regular employment. Although tradition may define certain positions within a company as full-time or part-time, being able to break with tradition and develop new ways to accommodate employees' desires to increase or reduce work hours can become yet another strategy for businesses to recruit and retain good workers.

About one in five employees spends at least part of his or her regular workweek working at home, while another seven percent say they would be allowed to do so.

> About one-quarter of wage and salaried employees currently are, or could choose to be, part of the telecommuting workforce.

- A surprising 19 percent of employees generally work at least part of their regularly scheduled hours at home, and 7 percent who are not currently working any regular hours at home say they would be allowed to do so (Table 6.1). Thus, about one-quarter of wage and salaried employees currently are, or could choose to be, part of the telecommuting workforce.

- Employees in smaller workplaces are more likely than those in larger workplaces to currently spend or be allowed to spend part of their regular workweek working at home—30 percent in small workplaces (fewer than 25 employees), 25 percent in medium-size workplaces (25 through 249 employees), and 22 percent in large workplaces (250 or more employees).

Table 6.1: Flexible Work Arrangements

Flexible Work Arrangement Items	Percentage (sample size)
Are you allowed to choose your own starting and quitting times within some range of hours?	(n=2872)
Yes	45%
No	55
Are you allowed to change your starting and quitting times on a daily basis?	(n=2856)
Yes	25%
No	75
Are you allowed to take a few days off to care for a sick child without losing pay, without using vacation days, and without having to make up some other reason for your absence? *(parents only)*	(n=1284)
Yes	50%
No	50
Are women who work for your employer able to take time off work to recuperate from childbirth without endangering their jobs?	(n=2658)
Yes	94%
No	6
Are men who work for your employer able to take time off work when they become fathers without endangering their jobs?	(n=2372)
Yes	80%
No	20
How hard is it for you to take time off during your workday to take care of personal or family matters?	(n=2833)
Not too hard, not at all hard	66%
Somewhat hard, very hard	34
I decide when I take breaks.	(n=2855)
Agree	73%
Disagree	27
If presently part-time, could you arrange to work full-time in your current position?	(n=412)
Yes or maybe	58%
No	42
If presently full-time, could you arrange to work part-time in your current position?	(n=2391)
Yes or maybe	38%
No	62
Currently work or would you be allowed to work at least part of regularly scheduled hours at home *(constructed from several items)*	(n=2877)
Currently work at least some regular hours at home	19%
Do not currently, but would be allowed to	7
Do not and could not	74

Workplace Environment

In our previous research,[1] we have found that support in the workplace—from supervisors, coworkers, and the work environment—is linked to employees' well-being as well as to job satisfaction, loyalty, and other outcomes of concern to employers. Such relationships have also been identified in the work of other researchers.[2] In this section of the report, we examine the various items that we used to measure workplace support. In Chapter 8, we will investigate the relationship between the workplace environment and indicators of job satisfaction, employee commitment, job performance, and retention.

Workers assessed the social environments in their workplaces by answering numerous questions about different facets of these environments. Answers to individual questions were combined to produce several general indicators of workplace support—*supportiveness of immediate supervisors*, *supportiveness of the workplace culture*, *quality of relationships with coworkers*, and *discrimination*—that are used in the analyses conducted in Chapter 8. Employees were also asked two independent questions: whether they are treated with *respect* at work and what the chances for advancement are for someone of their gender and racial or national origin—our indicator of *equal opportunity* in the workplace.

Most employees view their immediate supervisors as quite supportive, and supervisor supportiveness has increased somewhat since 1992.

- On all nine dimensions of supervisor support, large majorities of employees agree that their own immediate supervisors are supportive (Table 6.2).

- We find that employees interviewed in 1997 view their supervisors as somewhat more supportive than did employees interviewed five years earlier. Only one statement—"My supervisor accommodates me when I have personal or family business to take care of"—failed to elicit significantly higher levels of agreement in 1997 than in 1992.

- Although most of the differences between 1997 and 1992 are small in magnitude, taken as a whole they suggest a change in employees' perceptions that is presumably driven by actual increases in supervisor support over this interval. The most dramatic change is that more employees in 1997 (75.5 percent) than in 1992 (65.3 percent) feel comfortable bringing up personal and family issues with their supervisors—an increase of 10 percentage points.

---

1. Families and Work Institute (1993). *An Evaluation of Johnson & Johnson's Balancing Work and Family Program.* New York: Families and Work Institute.

    Galinsky, E. and Bond, J.T. (1996). Work and family: The Experiences of mothers and fathers in the U.S. Labor force. *The American Women 1996–97*. Edited by C. Costello and B. Kivimae Krimgold, 80–103. New York: W.W. Norton & Company.

2. Repetti, R.L., and Cosmas, K.A., (1991). The quality of the social environment at work and job satisfaction. *Journal of Applied Social Psychology*, 21: 840–854.

Table 6.2: Supervisor Support, 1997

Supervisor Support Items[a]	Percentage *(sample size)*[b]
My supervisor keeps me informed of the things I need to know to do my job well.	*(n=2553)*
Agree	87%
Disagree	13
My supervisor has expectations of my performance on the job that are realistic.	*(n=2551)*
Agree	92%
Disagree	8
My supervisor recognizes when I do a good job.	*(n=2553)*
Agree	89%
Disagree	11
My supervisor is supportive when I have a work problem.	*(n=2553)*
Agree	91%
Disagree	9
My supervisor is fair and doesn't show favoritism in responding to employees' personal or family needs.	*(n=2547)*
Agree	84%
Disagree	16
My supervisor accommodates me when I have family or personal business to take care of—for example, medical appointments, meeting with child's teacher, etc.	*(n=2520)*
Agree	94%
Disagree	6
My supervisor is understanding when I talk about personal or family issues that affect my work.	*(n=2396)*
Agree	91%
Disagree	9
I feel comfortable bringing up personal or family issues with my supervisor.	*(n=2461)*
Agree	76%
Disagree	24
My supervisor really cares about the effects that work demands have on my personal and family life.	*(n=2502)*
Agree	80%
Disagree	20

[a] *Responses to supervisor support items were dichotomized into two categories—agree vs. disagree—to simplify presentation and discussion. The full response scale is: strongly agree, somewhat agree, somewhat disagree, and strongly disagree.*

[b] *These items were only asked of respondents who said they had particular persons who were their immediate supervisors (n=2553).*

Two-thirds or more of employees view their workplace cultures as person- and family-friendly.

- As shown in Table 6.3, employees' disagreement with four *negative* statements about workplace culture ranges from 65 to 75 percent, which is to say they view their workplace cultures as supportive.

- The only significant change over the past five years is that employees interviewed in 1997 are less likely (29 percent)[3] than employees interviewed in 1992 (36 percent) to agree that there is an unwritten rule at work forbidding them to take care of family needs on company time.

Table 6.3: Workplace Culture

Workplace Culture Items [a]	Percentage (sample size)
There is an unwritten rule at my place of employment that you can't take care of family needs on company time.	(n=2850)
Agree	30%
Disagree	71
At my place of employment, employees who put their family or personal needs ahead of their jobs are not looked on favorably.	(n=2836)
Agree	35%
Disagree	65
If you have a problem managing your work and family responsibilities, the attitude at my place of employment is: "You made your bed, now lie in it!"	(n=2849)
Agree	25%
Disagree	75
At my place of employment, employees have to choose between advancing in their jobs or devoting attention to their family or personal lives.	(n=2824)
Agree	33%
Disagree	67

[a] *Responses to these items were dichotomized into two categories—agree vs. disagree—to simplify presentation and discussion. The full response scale is: strongly agree, somewhat agree, somewhat disagree, and strongly disagree.*

---

3. The slight difference in the percentage of employees agreeing with the statement in 1997 as reported here versus Table 6.3 is due to the fact that workers 65 and older are excluded from the full 1997 sample in 1997 versus 1992 comparisons in order to match the 1992 sample.

Employees in smaller workplaces view their workplace cultures as more person- and family-friendly than employees in larger workplaces do.

- Employees who work in smaller workplaces are more likely than employees at sites with more workers to view their workplaces as person- and family-friendly, with the exception of one item—"At my place of employment, employees who put their families or personal needs *ahead* [emphasis added] of their jobs are not looked on favorably"—for which we find no difference associated with workplace size.

- The largest difference appears in responses to the item stating that "At my place of employment, employees have to choose between advancing in their jobs or devoting attention to their family or personal lives." Seventy-three percent of employees in small workplaces (fewer than 25 employees) disagree with this statement, compared with 67 percent in medium-size workplaces (25 through 249 employees) and 59 percent in large workplaces (250 or more employees).

Most employees have positive relationships with coworkers.

- Ninety-one percent of employees feel that they are a part of the group of people they work with, and 89 percent look forward to being with the people they work with each day (Table 6.4). We found no differences between the 1992 and 1997 samples on either of these items.

Table 6.4 Relationships with Coworkers

Coworker Relationship Items [a]	Percentage (sample size)
I feel I am really a part of the group of people I work with.	(n=2869)
Agree	91%
Disagree	9
I look forward to being with the people I work with each day.	(n=2865)
Agree	89%
Disagree	11

[a] *Responses to these items were dichotomized into two categories—agree vs. disagree—to simplify presentation and discussion. The full response scale is: strongly agree, somewhat agree, somewhat disagree, and strongly disagree.*

Men are slightly more confident than women that employees of their same gender and racial or national background can advance in the organizations where they work.

- Workers were asked to rate the chances for advancement in their current workplaces for a man (if respondent was a man) or woman (if respondent was a woman) of their same racial or national origin. As shown in Table 6.5, men are more confident that male employees like themselves can advance in their organizations than women are that female employees like themselves can.

Non-minority employees have much more confidence than minority employees that workers of their own gender and racial or national background can advance.

- More striking than the previous finding for men and women is the difference in the ratings made by minority and non-minority workers. Non-minority employees are much more confident than minority employees that workers of their own gender and racial or ethnic background can advance in their organizations. Thirty percent of non-minority employees, versus 20 percent of minority employees, rate the chance for someone of their gender and race or national origin to advance as excellent, and 38 percent of non-minority employees rate the chance for advancement as good, compared with 32 percent of minority employees.

Table 6.5: Equal Opportunity for Advancement by Gender and Ethnicity

Equal Opportunity	Total Percentage (sample size)	Men	Sig.	Women	Non-Minority	Sig.	Minority
How would you rate the chance to advance in your organization for a man/woman of your race or national origin?	(n=2844)	(n=1478)	*	(n=1366)	(n=2256)	***	(n=563)
Poor	12%	11%		14%	11%		18%
Fair	23	24		23	22		30
Good	37	36		37	38		32
Excellent	28	30		26	30		20

Significance: $* = p < .01$; $*** = p < .0001$.

Almost one in five employees feels that he or she has been discriminated against on the job because of age, gender, or race.

- As shown in Figure 6.2, 7 percent of employees feel discriminated against at their current jobs because of age, 10 percent because of sex, and 7 percent because of race or national origin. Eighteen percent of employees feel they have been discriminated against in one or more of these ways.

  Although it is troublesome to find that nearly one-fifth of employees have experienced discrimination over the entire course of their work lives, it is particularly disconcerting to think that so many employees continue working in places where they feel discriminated against. Quite apart from the question of whether these employees have any legal grounds for their claims, the *feeling* of discrimination in itself can be damaging to employees' well-being as well as to their attitudes and behavior on the job.

- Not surprisingly, women are more likely (14 percent) than men (5 percent) to report sex discrimination, while minority employees are more likely (20 percent) than non-minority workers (4 percent) to feel discriminated against because of race or national origin. Supplemental analyses also reveal that feelings of age discrimination vary significantly by age groups. Perhaps counterintuitively, employees under 30 years old report the highest level of age discrimination (12 percent), with four percent of 30- through 39-year-olds, 6 percent of 40- through 49-year-olds, and nine percent of those 50 years and older feeling discriminated against by age.

> Employees under 30 years old report the highest level of age discrimination (12 percent), with four percent of 30- through 39-year-olds, 6 percent of 40- through 49-year-olds, and nine percent of those 50 years and older feeling discriminated against by age.

Perceived discrimination on the job has remained the same over the past 20 years.

- The proportions of employees reporting discrimination on the job by age, sex, and race or national origin have remained the same since 1977.

Figure 6.2: Do you feel in anyway discriminated against on your job because of your age ... because you are a man or woman ... because of your race or national origin?

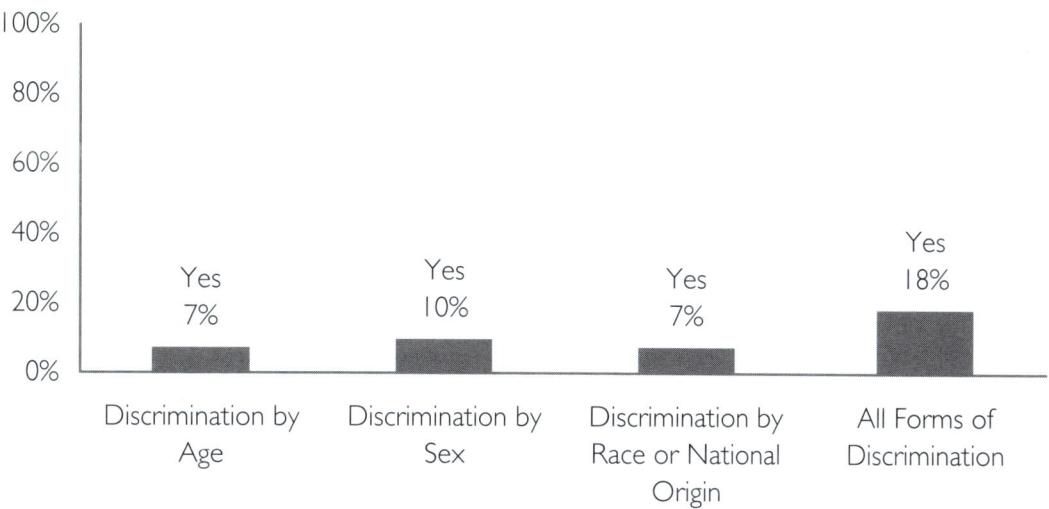

Despite some signs of perceived inequality of opportunity and discrimination on the job, most workers feel they are treated with respect at work.

- Ninety-one percent of employees agree somewhat (27 percent) or strongly (64 percent) that they are treated with respect at the companies or organizations where they work.

- While our findings reveal no differences between men and women, or between minority and non-minority employees, employees in non-professional/non-managerial jobs are somewhat less likely (90 percent) than employees in management and professional jobs (94 percent) to agree somewhat or strongly that they feel respected at their workplaces.

Table 6.6: Respect Received at Work

Respect	Percentage (sample size)
At the company or organization where I work, I am treated with respect.	(n=2872)
Strongly agree	64%
Somewhat agree	27
Somewhat disagree	5
Strongly disagree	4

As previously noted in this report, the fact that the majority of employees in the labor force are satisfied, supported, respected, and so forth does not mean there is nothing to be concerned about. For example, a minority of 36 percent of employees—more than 40 million wage and salaried workers in the U.S. labor force—do *not* strongly agree that they are treated with respect where they work. Moreover, the proportion of workers who feel respected in any given workplace may be significantly higher or lower than this average for the workforce as a whole.

7 Employee Outcomes on the Job

Recruitment, productivity, and retention have become a corporate mantra in the '90s. And tight labor markets at home, exacerbated by growing competition abroad, make these issues more compelling every day. In this chapter, we describe the indicators of employee productivity and retention that are incorporated in the conceptual model: job satisfaction, commitment to employer, job performance, and retention. In Chapter 8, we will explore the links between these outcome indicators and other elements in the model: characteristics of individual employees, characteristics of their lives off the job, aspects of their personal well-being, and characteristics of their jobs and workplaces.

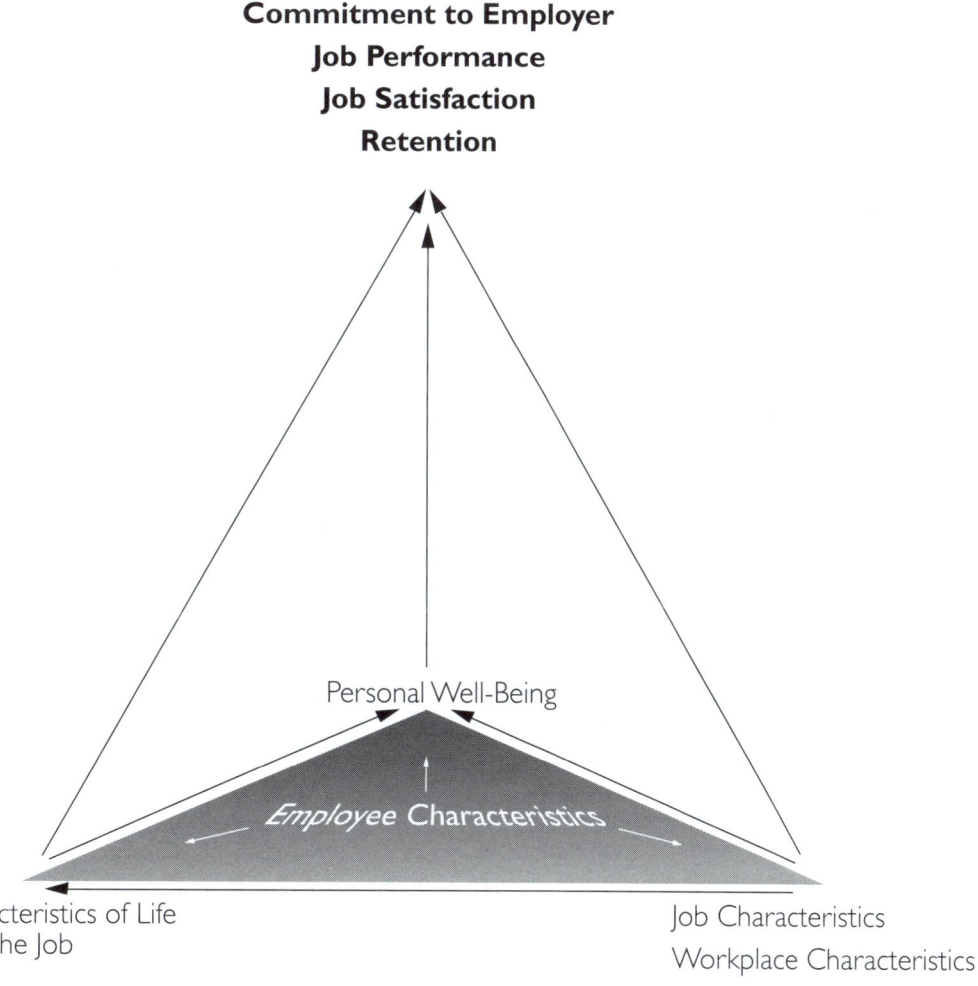

Although objective measures of recruitment, productivity, and retention can be obtained only through independent observations in the workplace, there are good reasons to believe that employee surveys can provide valid indicators of productivity and retention. First, in evaluating efforts to affect these outcomes, companies rely heavily on internal surveys of employees. Second, small-scale research confirms that various measures from surveys do, indeed, predict behavioral outcomes of interest—and sometimes even such bottom-line outcomes as revenue growth and operating margins.[1] What is more, data from large-scale surveys of representative samples of U.S. employees are particularly effective at capturing the full range of variability in the nation's employees and workplaces, enabling generalizations to be made about employees and employers at large.

Our 1997 survey asked several questions related to job satisfaction, commitment, retention, and productivity. Employees' responses to these questions represent the outcomes we attempt to predict in Chapter 8, guided by the conceptual model presented in Chapter 1.

Employees are generally satisfied with their jobs—somewhat more so today than 20 years ago.

- As shown in Figure 7.1, 91 percent of employees are somewhat (44 percent) or very (47 percent) satisfied with their jobs in general terms. In addition, 69 percent (Figure 7.2) say they would take the same job again without hesitation. Although this represents a generally high level of job satisfaction, there remains plenty of room for improvement, since only 47 percent are very satisfied at present.

Figure 7.1: General Satisfaction with Job

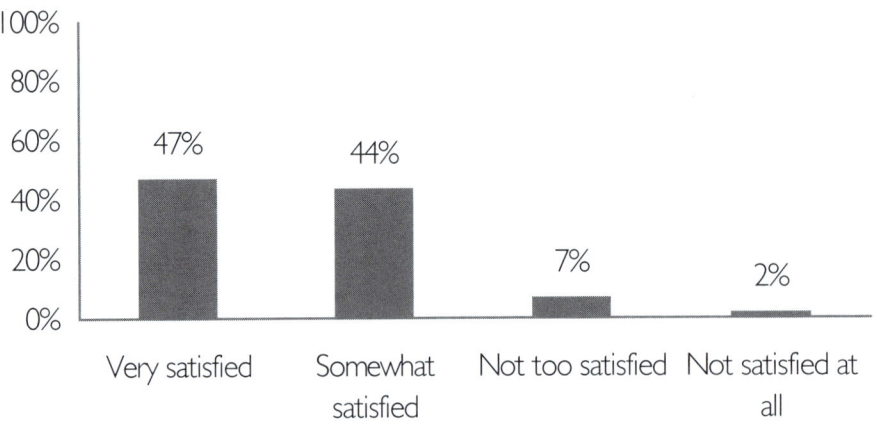

---

1. For example: Rucci, A.J., Kirn, S.P., and Quinn, R.T. (1998). The employee-customer profit chain at Sears. *Harvard Business Review*, 76: 83–97.

Figure 7.2: Knowing What You Now Know, If You Had to Decide All Over Again, Would You Take the Same Job?

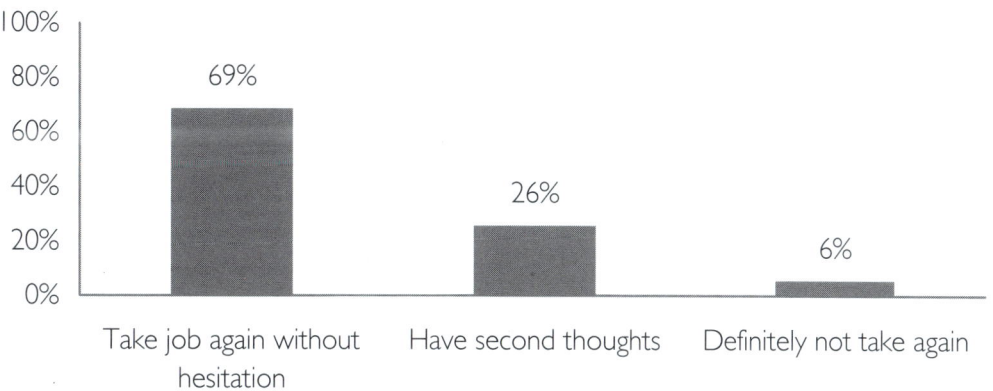

- Comparing 1997 with 1977, we find that employees have become slightly more satisfied with their jobs over the past twenty years.[2] For general job satisfaction, there is a four percentage point increase from 1977 to 1997 in the proportion of employees responding that they are very or somewhat satisfied. There is a five percentage point increase for employees saying they would take the same job again without hesitation.

  Most employees are also committed to the success of their companies and loyal to their employers, despite the flagging loyalty of employers to their employees.

- Ninety-one percent of employees agree somewhat (36 percent) or strongly (55 percent) that they are willing to work harder than they have to in order to help their employers succeed. And 73 percent describe themselves as very loyal (42 percent) or extremely loyal (31 percent) to their employers. (Table 7.1)

> There is a four percentage point increase from 1977 to 1997 in the proportion of employees responding that they are very or somewhat satisfied with their jobs.

---

2. For purposes of comparison, the 1997 sample was reduced to employees working 20 or more hours per week and interviewed in English, while the 1977 sample was reduced to employees 18 and older.

Employee Outcomes on the Job

Table 7.1: Commitment to Helping Company Succeed and Loyalty to Employer

Commitment and Loyalty	Percentage (sample size)
Commitment to Success of Company:	(n=2875)
I am willing to work harder than I have to, to help my company or organization succeed.	
Strongly disagree	3%
Somewhat disagree	6
Somewhat agree	36
Strongly agree	55
Loyalty:	(n=2872)
How loyal do you feel to your employer?	
Not loyal at all	2%
Not very loyal	2
Somewhat loyal	23
Very loyal	42
Extremely loyal	31

More than three of five employees plan to stay with their current employers for at least the next year, while only 15 percent are highly motivated to move on—proportions that have not changed in the past two decades.

- Sixty-two percent of employees say it is not at all likely they "will make a genuine effort to find a new job with another employer within the next year," while 22 percent say it is somewhat likely, and 15 percent say it is very likely. (Figure 7.3)

Figure 7.3: How Likely Is It You Will Make a Genuine Effort to Find a New Job with Another Employer in the Next Year?

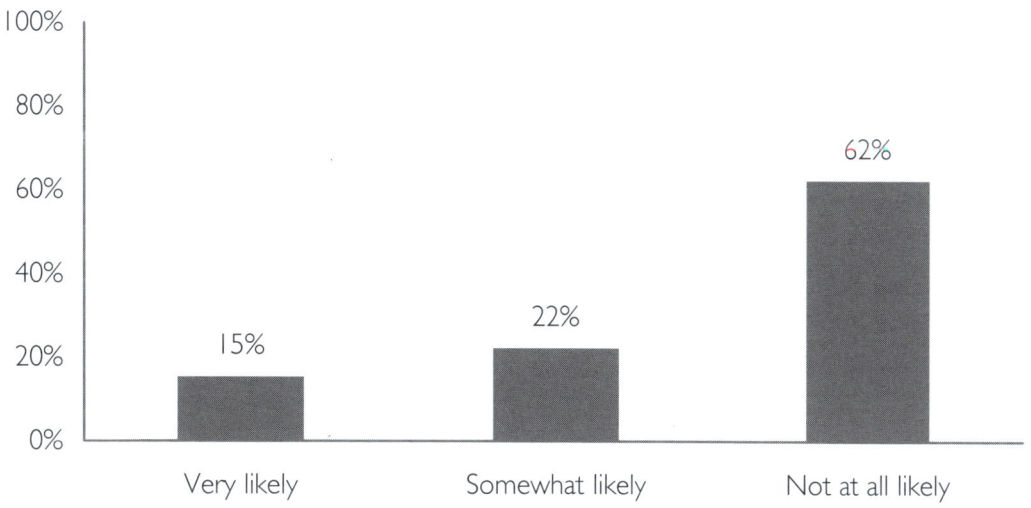

- Comparing 1997 with 1977, we find no change over the past 20 years in the likelihood that employees will seek new jobs with other employers in the next year.[3] Although the implied contract between employers and employees—a lifetime job for lifetime loyalty—may be a thing of the past, it appears that most employees continue to find stable employment preferable to job–hopping. This is not to say, however, that employees would refuse attractive job offers from competing companies.

If retention of employees, as measured by their plans to leave, has not changed in the past two decades for the wage and salaried labor force as a whole, why is retention such a prominent concern these days? The cost of recruitment in tight labor markets is surely one reason, particularly regarding highly skilled workers who are in short supply. A more pervasive and lasting reason, however, may be the growing human capital costs of turnover as even entry-level jobs become more challenging and employers invest more time and money in developing the skills of new hires.

> Although the implied contract between employers and employees—a lifetime job for lifetime loyalty—may be a thing of the past, it appears that most employees continue to find stable employment preferable to job–hopping.

---

3. For purposes of comparison, the 1997 sample was reduced to employees working 20 or more hours per week and interviewed in English, while the 1977 sample was reduced to employees 18 and older.

For most employees, personal life off the job has little negative impact on productivity at work. However, for some, the impact is substantial and no doubt bothersome to employees, supervisors, and coworkers alike.

- In response to the five home-to-job spillover questions presented in Table 7.2, the majority of employees indicate that their personal lives never or only rarely have negative effects on their work productivity. Comparable data are not available from 1977.

- Negative spillover from home to job is greatest for the last question in the series, in which one–third of employees indicate that their personal lives keep them from concentrating on their jobs sometimes or more often. In addition, 28 percent of employees indicate that life off the job drained them of the energy they needed to do their jobs sometimes or more often. Both of these questions tap psychological states that may or may not be reflected in ultimate productivity or even in behavior that is observed by coworkers and supervisors.

> One–third of employees indicate that their personal lives keep them from concentrating on their jobs sometimes or more frequently.

These findings reveal that most employees manage to keep their personal lives from affecting their job performance most of the time. Even a visual comparison of job-to-home spillover findings in Table 4.3 of Chapter 4 with home-to-job spillover findings in Table 7.2 (below) suggests that spillover from work into the personal lives of employees far exceeds spillover from their personal lives into their work, and statistical tests on global spillover indices confirm this difference. The relationship between job-to-home and home-to-job spillover will be explored further in Chapter 8.

Table 7.2: Home-to-Job Spillover Affecting Productivity

Outcomes	Percentage *(sample size)*
In the past three months ...	*(n=2869)*
How often has your family or personal life kept you from getting work done on time at your job?	
Never	44%
Rarely	39
Sometimes	13
Often	2
Very often	2
How often has your family or personal life kept you from taking on extra work at your job?	*(n=2872)*
Never	43%
Rarely	33
Sometimes	14
Often	6
Very often	3
How often has your family or personal life kept you from doing as good a job at work as you could?	*(n=2871)*
Never	44%
Rarely	40
Sometimes	13
Often	2
Very often	2
How often has your family or personal life drained you of the energy you needed to do your job?	*(n=2874)*
Never	35%
Rarely	37
Sometimes	21
Often	5
Very often	2
How often has your family or personal life kept you from concentrating on your job?	*(n=2872)*
Never	27%
Rarely	41
Sometimes	27
Often	4
Very often	2

8 What Can Employers Do to Improve Satisfaction, Commitment, Performance, and Retention?

The findings presented in this chapter point to an important conclusion and message for business: Assuming that pay and fringe benefits are competitive, the most effective way to improve employee attitudes, performance, and retention is to create better-quality jobs and more supportive workplaces, while keeping job demands at reasonable levels.

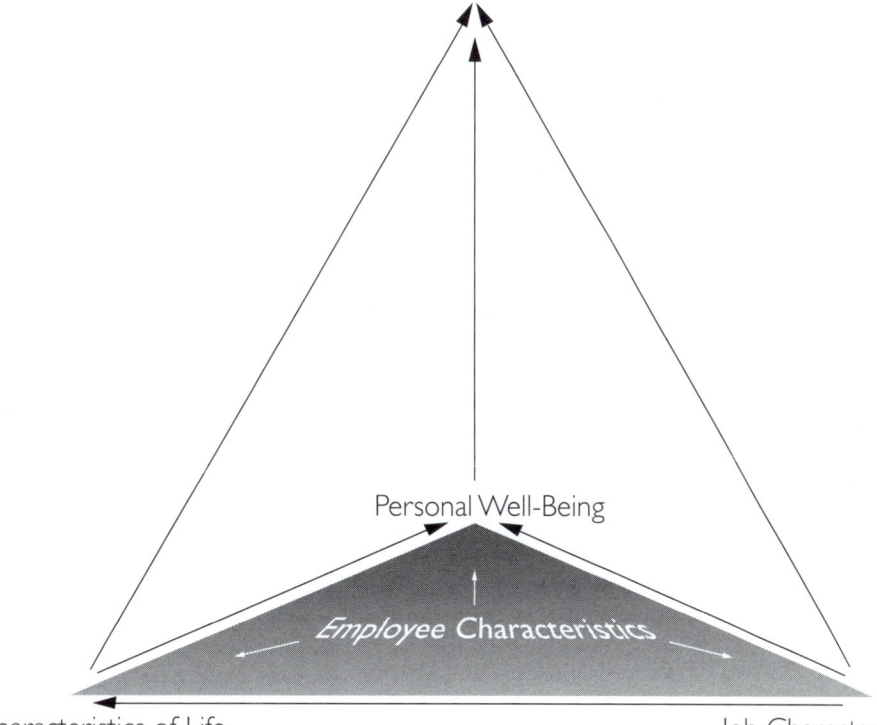

We believe that the findings presented in this chapter provide a sound basis for inferences about what employers might do to improve employee commitment, productivity, and retention. This is particularly so when findings are viewed through the lens of the conceptual model presented in Chapter 1. Throughout this chapter, emphasis is placed on identifying job and workplace characteristics that are within employers' power to modify in order to improve business outcomes.

Chapter 8 is divided into five sections, each addressing one of the employee outcomes described in Chapter 7—*job satisfaction*, *commitment to employer's success*, *loyalty*, *retention*, and *productivity* as it is affected by life off the job. We conducted analyses to identify which factors explain or predict particular outcomes. The potential explanatory factors examined in these analyses are described in Chapters 2 through 6 of the report—*employee demographics*, *characteristics of life off the job*, *personal well-being*, *job characteristics*, and general *workplace characteristics*.

> Employers who provide higher-quality jobs and more supportive workplaces will have a competitive edge.

Explanation of Terminology and Methods

In the sections that follow, we conduct analyses to *explain the variability*, or differences, in job satisfaction, loyalty, job performance, and retention among employees.[4] Although the statistics are fairly complicated, the concept behind these analyses is simple. For example, as a group, the several factors labeled "employee demographics" in Chapter 2 explain about 3 percent of the total variability in job satisfaction. If these factors explained 100 percent of the variability in job satisfaction, one could "theoretically" build a workforce of completely satisfied employees by simply hiring and keeping employees with particular demographic characteristics. In reality, however, such a strategy is neither feasible nor legal. Anyway, much more variability in job satisfaction than that explained by employee demographics (3 percent) remains to be explained by other factors (97 percent).

In all of the analyses in this chapter, we treat employee demographics as given, and hold them constant or *control for* them when evaluating the explanatory power of other factors—*characteristics of life off the job* (Chapter 3), *job characteristics* (Chapter 5), and *workplace characteristics* (Chapter 6). Controlling for employee demographics simply means

---

4. Multiple linear regression analysis was used to evaluate the relative explanatory power of different sets of factors—employee demographics, compensation and benefits, job demands, job quality, and workplace support. Analyses first controlled for demographic factors, then evaluated the contributions of other sets of factors independently. Unweighted data were used in regressions. All statements about the relationships between individual factors and dependent variables are based on partial correlations controlling for demographic factors, except in the case of demographics themselves where bivariate correlations with dependent variables are used.

determining how much variability is explained by other factors *in addition to* the variability explained by demographic factors.

After conducting exploratory analyses that examined relationships among all major components of the conceptual model, we decided for purposes of this section to focus on job and workplace characteristics as predictors of employee outcomes. Characteristics of life off the job (Chapter 3) explained very little of the variability (2 through 3 percent as a group) in job satisfaction, commitment to helping company succeed, loyalty, and retention. Likewise, indicators of personal well-being (Chapter 4) were weakly predictive of outcomes (0.3 through 3 percent as a group) after controlling for job and workplace characteristics. Only in the case of job performance, as measured by home-to-job spillover, do we present findings related to all major components of the conceptual model.

Job Satisfaction

Wages and fringe benefits are often considered primary determinants of job satisfaction. However, findings from the survey tell a different story. The quality of employees' jobs—autonomy, learning opportunities, meaningfulness, opportunities for advancement, job security—and the supportiveness of their work environments—flexibility, supervisor support, supportive workplace culture, positive coworker relations, respect, and equal opportunity—are far more important predictors of job satisfaction than earnings and benefits.

Employee demographics—gender, age, race/ethnicity, education, years in labor force, and occupation—explain 3 percent of the variability in job satisfaction among wage and salaried workers. Before conducting analyses of other potential explanatory factors, we first controlled for the variability in job satisfaction explained by employee demographics.

Compensation and access to fringe benefits do little to explain job satisfaction.

- As a group, employees' hourly earnings, access to traditional fringe benefits (health insurance, pensions, paid vacation, etc.), and access to dependent-care benefits (child care resource and referral, on- or near-site child care, elder care resource and referral, etc.) explain only 2 percent of the variability in job satisfaction among wage and salaried workers. Of the three individual factors, only traditional and dependent-care benefits are independently related to job satisfaction, while hourly earnings has no explanatory power.

> The quality of employees' jobs and the supportiveness of their work environments are far more important predictors of job satisfaction than earnings and benefits.

This finding should not be interpreted as meaning that pay is unimportant to employees' feelings about their jobs. As reported below, opportunities for advancement and opportunities that are equal to those of other workers have significant impact on job satisfaction. However, assuming that wages are competitive and employees are treated fairly in pay decisions and promotions, pay in itself does not appear to be related to job satisfaction. Also, note (Chapter 5) that we have measured access to benefits, not their utilization. It may well be that access to dependent care benefits, for example, have a much stronger positive effect on job satisfaction among employees who actually use them.

Employees whose jobs are more demanding are slightly less satisfied with their jobs than other workers are.

Job demands are represented by the following factors: all paid and unpaid hours worked per week at main or only job; number of nights away from home on business during the past three months; frequency of required overtime with little or no notice; regular daytime shift versus other schedule; frequency of bringing work home; and an index of job pressures that combines responses to several items from the questionnaire, such as having to work very hard or very fast. (See Chapter 5.)

- As a group, the job-demand factors explain 3 percent of the variability in job satisfaction, with more required overtime with little or no notice and higher job pressures being the only individual factors that have significant explanatory power. As these demands increase, satisfaction decreases.

Employees with better quality jobs are much more satisfied with their jobs than other workers are.

Job quality includes job autonomy, learning opportunities on the job, meaningfulness of job, opportunities for advancement on job, and job security.

- As a group, factors measuring the quality of employees' jobs have very substantial explanatory power, accounting for 32 percent of the variability in job satisfaction among wage and salaried workers. All five components of job quality are positively related to job satisfaction. That is, as job quality increases, so does satisfaction.

Employees in supportive workplace environments are the most satisfied with their jobs.

Workplace climate and support is represented by the following factors: flexibility; supervisor support; supportive workplace culture; positive coworker relations; equal opportunities for advancement by workers of the same gender and race/national origin as respondent; lack of discrimination by age, gender, and race/national origin; and respect received in the workplace.

- Employees who work in environments that are broadly supportive, respectful, fair, and responsive to their individual needs—as persons with lives off the job—are most satisfied with their jobs. As a group, workplace—support factors explain 37 percent of the variability in employees' job satisfaction, and all of these factors are positively related to satisfaction. As support increases, so does satisfaction.

    Characteristics of jobs and workplaces are related to job satisfaction in the same way for hourly as well as salaried workers.

- Demographic factors, earnings and fringe benefits, job demands, job quality, and workplace support are related to job satisfaction in the same way for hourly (non-exempt) as well as salaried (exempt) employees. Moreover, the relative explanatory power of these factors is nearly identical across groups. For hourly and salaried workers, having a high quality job and a supportive workplace are far and away the most powerful factors accounting for job satisfaction.

> Employees who work in environments that are broadly supportive, respectful, fair, and responsive to their individual needs—as persons with lives off the job—are most satisfied with their jobs.

Summary of major findings

Figure 8.1: Job Satisfaction: Relative Explanatory Power of Different Job and Workplace Factors

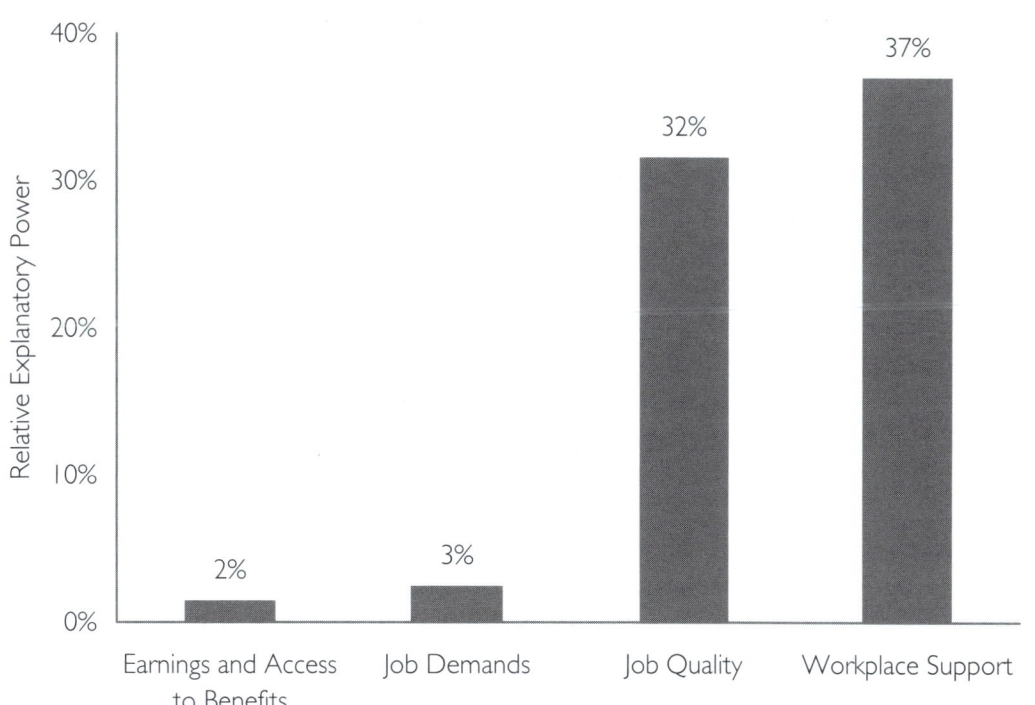

Commitment to Helping Company Succeed

Every employer would like to have employees who are willing to work harder than required to help the company succeed. Findings from the survey reveal that employers who develop better-quality jobs and more supportive workplace environments may also encourage employees to become more committed to the success of the company. Earnings and fringe benefits, on the other hand, are unrelated to commitment.

Employee demographics do not explain any significant proportion of the variability in employees' commitments to company success, as measured by their "willingness to work harder than they have to in order to help their company succeed." Nevertheless, analyses of other potential explanatory factors—compensation and benefits, job demands, job quality, and workplace support—replicate the analytic model used throughout this chapter by first controlling for employee demographics.

Neither pay nor access to fringe benefits, in itself, is related to employees' commitments to helping their companies succeed.

Job demands are weakly related to employees' commitments to helping their companies succeed. In this instance, employees who are more committed to their employers' success may make their jobs somewhat more demanding by working longer hours and taking on greater responsibilities.

As noted in the introduction to this chapter, cross-sectional survey data do not permit firm conclusions about what causes what. In the case of job demands, three of six factors are significantly related to employees' commitments to company success—number of hours worked, frequency of bringing work home from the job, and job pressures—with greater demands being associated with greater commitment. Common sense would suggest that working harder and faster is affected by commitment, rather than the other way around.

- Job demands do not help explain the variability in employees' commitments to helping their companies succeed but, rather, provide evidence of such commitment. That is, employees who are more committed tend to take on more responsibility and work harder.

Employees with better-quality jobs are more committed to helping their employers succeed than other workers are.

- As a group, the factors representing job quality—autonomy, learning opportunities, meaningfulness of work, security, and opportunities for advancement—explain 11 percent of the variability in employees' willingness to work harder than they have to in order to help their employers succeed. All five job-quality factors are positively related to commitment, with job autonomy, learning opportunities, and meaningfulness having the greatest explanatory power.

Similarly, employees with more supportive workplaces are more willing than other workers to work harder than they have to in order to help their employers succeed.

Workplace support is represented by the following factors: flexibility; supervisor support; supportive workplace culture; positive coworker relations; equal opportunities for advancement by workers of the same gender and race/national origin as respondent; lack of discrimination by age, gender, and race/national origin; and respect received in the workplace.

- Employees who work in environments that are broadly supportive, respectful, fair, and responsive to their individual needs—as people with lives off the job—are the most committed to helping their employers succeed. Workplace-support factors explain 11 percent of the variability in employees' job satisfaction, and all workplace-support factors are positively related to commitment.

> For both hourly and salaried employees, higher job quality and workplace support are associated with employees' willingness to work harder than necessary to help their companies succeed.

Findings for hourly and salaried employees are quite similar.

- For both hourly (nonexempt) and salaried (exempt) employees, higher job quality and workplace support are associated with employees' willingness to work harder than necessary to help their companies succeed.

Summary of major findings

Figure 8.2: Commitment to Company Success: Relative Explanatory Power of Different Job and Workplace Factors

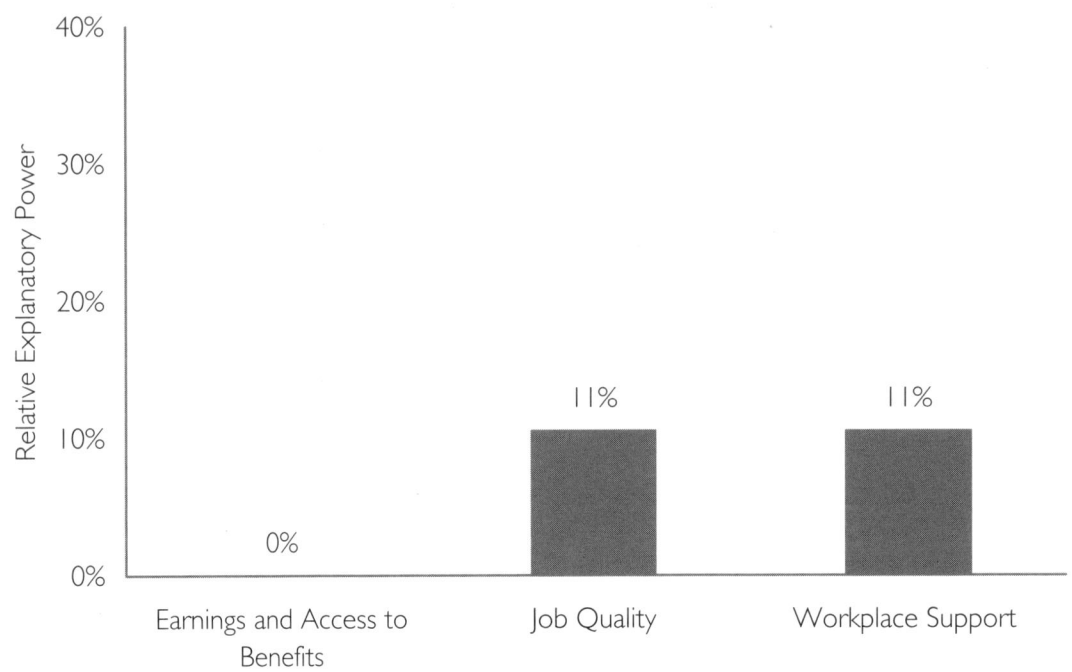

Loyalty to Employer

In recent years, widespread downsizing has called into question the whole notion of company loyalty. After all, if employers are not loyal to their employees, why should they imagine that employees will be loyal to them? Nonetheless, most employers still place high value on a loyal workforce, and findings from the survey suggest that providing a high-quality job and a more supportive workplace may be the most effective way to win a worker's loyalty.

Employee demographics explain only 2 percent of the variability in employees' loyalty to their employers. Before conducting analyses of other potential explanatory factors, we first controlled for the variability in loyalty explained by employee demographics.

Earnings and fringe benefits, in themselves, have almost no relationship to employees' loyalty to their employers.

- Earnings and access to traditional and dependent care benefits explain less than 1 percent of the variability in loyalty among wage and salaried workers.

Job demands are only weakly related to loyalty, and what relationship exists suggests that more loyal employees may place greater demands on themselves.

- In the case of job demands, only frequency of bringing work home from the job is related to loyalty, with a higher incidence of bringing work home being associated with greater loyalty. Common sense would suggest that loyalty affects this job-demand factor, rather than the over way around. That is, employees who are more loyal are more likely to bring work home.

Employees with better quality jobs are considerably more loyal to their employers than other workers are.

- As a group, job-quality factors—autonomy, learning opportunities, meaningfulness of work, security, and opportunities for advancement—explain 19 percent of the variability in employees' loyalty to their employers. All five job-quality factors are positively related to loyalty, with similar explanatory power. As job quality increases so does loyalty.

> As workplace supportiveness increases, so does loyalty.

Employees whose workplaces are supportive and responsive to their individual needs are the most loyal.

Workplace support is represented by the following: flexibility; supervisor support; supportive workplace culture; positive coworker relations; equal opportunities for advancement by workers of the same gender and race/national origin as respondent; lack of discrimination by age, gender, and race/national origin; and respect received in the workplace.

- Having a flexible, supportive, fair, and respectful workplace makes a big difference in the loyalty employees feel toward their employers. Indeed, workplace support explains 24 percent of the variability in employees' loyalty. All component factors are positively related to loyalty, with similar explanatory power. In short, as workplace supportiveness increases, so does loyalty.

   This pattern of findings holds for hourly as well as salaried workers.

- A high-quality job and supportive workplace are equally important to the loyalty of hourly (nonexempt) and salaried (exempt) employees.

Summary of major findings

Figure 8.3: Loyalty to Employer: Relative Explanatory Power of Different Job and Workplace Factors

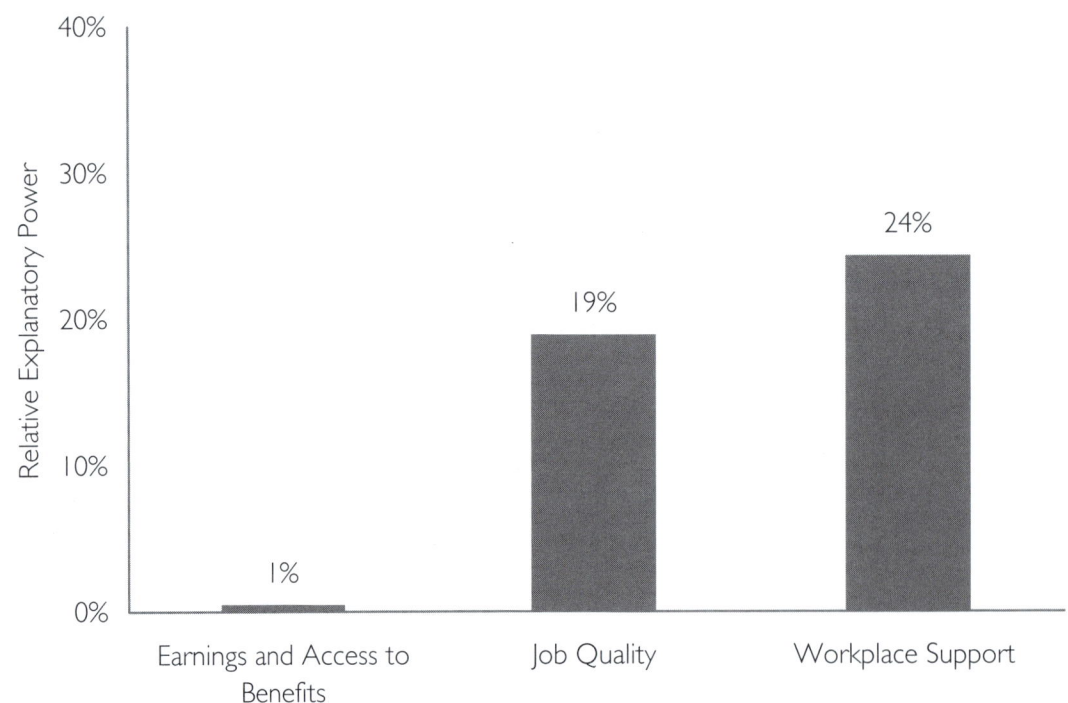

Employee Retention

When labor markets are tight, companies large and small are greatly concerned with, and sometimes bewildered by, the question of how best to retain employees. Although employees remain with or leave their employers for many reasons that have nothing to do with their jobs or workplaces, findings from the survey reveal that employees with better-quality jobs and more supportive workplaces are more likely than other workers to plan on remaining with their current employers. In contrast, earnings are unrelated to retention, while access to fringe benefits and job demands are only weakly related.

We measured employee retention, or the likelihood of retention for at least one year, by asking, "Taking everything into consideration, how likely is it that you will make a genuine effort to find a new job with another employer within the next year?"

- Employee demographics explain 7 percent of the variability in retention, which, though still a modest amount, is two to three times more than these factors explain in the variability of other outcomes. Of the six demographic factors examined, only age and race/ethnicity are significantly related to retention. Younger workers and minority workers are more likely than others to want to find a new job with another employer within the next year.

> Employees with better-quality jobs and more supportive workplaces are more likely than other workers to plan on remaining with their current employers.

Fringe benefits, but not earnings, are weakly related to employees' intentions to remain with their employers.

- As a group, earnings and fringe benefits explain 4 percent of the variability in retention. Although earnings, which are presumably competitive with market rates in most instances, are unrelated to retention, access to traditional fringe benefits and dependent-care benefits are. Access to traditional fringe benefits, which includes health insurance for worker and family, is most predictive.

Job demands are also weakly related to retention.

- As a group, job-demand factors explain only 2 percent of the variability in retention. Of the six factors included in job demands, three have significant explanatory power. Employees who work longer hours, who are more frequently required to work overtime with little or no notice, and who work something other than a standard daytime shift are slightly more likely than other employees to say they want to find work with another employer.

Employees with better-quality jobs are substantially more likely than other employees to plan on staying with their current employers.

- Job quality explains 16 percent of the variability in retention as measured by the likelihood that employees will remain with their current employers for at least a year. All five components of job quality—autonomy, learning opportunities, meaningfulness of job, job security, and personal opportunities for advancement—are positively related to retention. Job security has the greatest explanatory power, followed by learning opportunities and personal opportunities for advancement. That is, as job quality increases, so does retention.

Employees whose workplaces are more supportive and responsive to their individual needs are also more likely than other workers to be retained.

- As a group, workplace-support factors explain 10 percent of the variability in retention. All seven workplace factors—flexibility, supervisor support, workplace culture, coworker relations, equal opportunity, lack of discrimination, and respect—are positively related to retention.

The pattern of findings is similar for hourly as well as salaried workers.

Summary of major findings

Figure 8.4: Retention: Relative Explanatory Power of Different Job and Workplace Factors

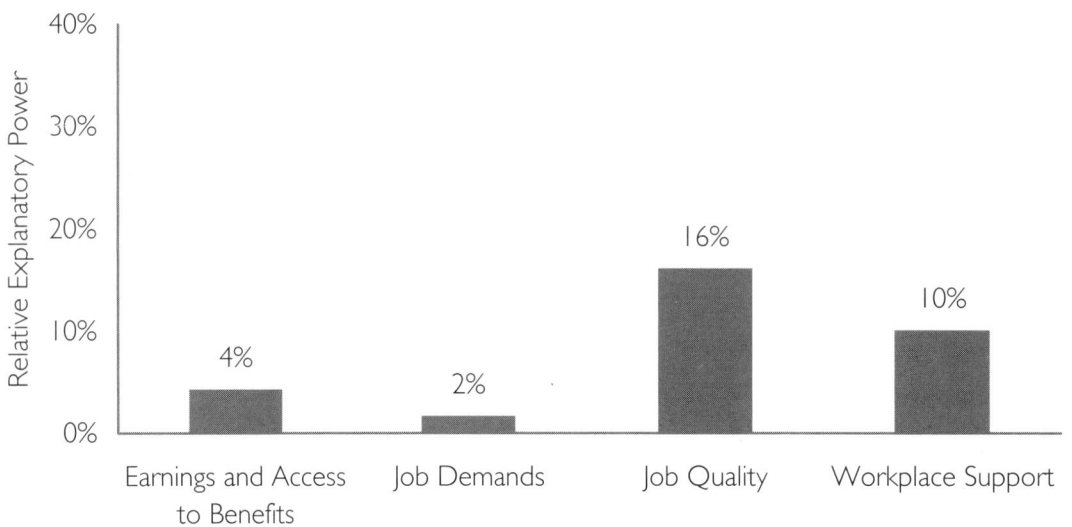

Job Performance

Job performance is affected by many things, including spillover from problems that employees have in their personal lives. To improve job performance, employers frequently offer special work-life programs—wellness programs, employee assistance programs, child and elder care information and referral services, direct child care services, and so forth—to help employees solve personal problems so they will not spill over into the workplace and reduce productivity. Such strategies generally treat employees' personal problems as products of their lives off the job and unrelated to their work lives.

Our findings, however, indicate that work life is actually an important source of employees' personal problems. That is, spillover from jobs into workers' personal lives can create or exacerbate problems off the job that, in turn, spill over into work and diminish productivity. Thus, helping employees solve problems in their personal lives by providing special programs of assistance, without also reducing the extent to which jobs contribute to these problems, may severely limit the impact of work-life programs on job performance.

Based on our findings, the negative spillover effects that demanding and hectic jobs can have on the quality of workers' personal lives and well-being are of particular concern. When job demands exceed some individually defined level, it seems that not even the most supportive workplace can protect workers from negative job spillover into their personal lives. This spillover is reflected in high stress levels, poor coping, bad moods, and insufficient time and energy available for important people in employees' lives—creating "problems" that spill over into work and impair job performance. Therefore, employers' actions not only toward increasing the supportiveness of workplaces, but also toward urging and helping employees "get a life" off the job may be crucial to improving employee productivity over the long run—not to mention the obvious benefits to workers and their families.

> Actions by employers to urge and help employees to "get a life" off the job may be crucial to improving employee productivity over the long run.

In this section, we use as our indicator of job performance employees' self-admissions of the extent to which job performance was negatively affected by personal and family life during the preceding three months. Five items (Chapter 7)—frequency of not getting work done on time, not taking on extra work, not doing as good a job at work as they could, being drained of energy needed to do job, and not being able to concentrate on job because of family or personal life—were combined into a single index. While this index does not provide a comprehensive and independent measure of job performance, which is only possible through direct observation, it does capture a dimension of performance that is particularly relevant to the themes of this report. In the remainder of this section, we will refer to this indicator of job performance as *home-to-job spillover*.

In examining the relationships between personal life and work life, we apply the conceptual model presented in Chapter 1 rather differently than we do in the preceding sections of this chapter. One expects, of course, that various aspects of employees' personal lives—such as having to deal with time demands, general stress factors, and specific problems associated with child or elder care—are likely to affect spillover from home to job. Thus, the explanatory model shown in Figure 8.5 incorporates *characteristics of life off the job* (Chapter 3) as primary explanatory factors.

Based on previous research, we also expected that many employees would experience spillover from work into their lives off the job that increases their stress levels while depressing their moods, diminishing energy levels, and hampering coping abilities as well as leaving them with insufficient time for the people most important to them. All of these effects might, in turn, be associated with higher levels of spillover from home to job. We selected two measures to capture job spillover effects: *job burnout* and *job-to-home spillover*. These multi-item indicators—for example, frequency of feeling emotionally drained from work, feeling burned-out or stressed by work, not having enough energy to do things with family or other important people because of job, and so forth—are described in Chapter 4 as job-related measures of personal well-being. They are strongly correlated with our general measures of personal well-being—stress, coping, and life satisfaction (Chapter 4)—but are more robust for purposes of our explanatory analyses and have the advantage of being directly linked to work in the minds of employees.

Finally, we expected that *job and workplace characteristics* would be strong predictors of job burnout and spillover and have an *indirect* impact on spillover from home to job by way of their impact on personal well-being. Figure 8.5 depicts this hypothesis as a causal chain, leading from job and workplace characteristics to burnout and job spillover, then to spillover from home to job.

Figure 8.5: Model Explaining Home-to-Job Spillover

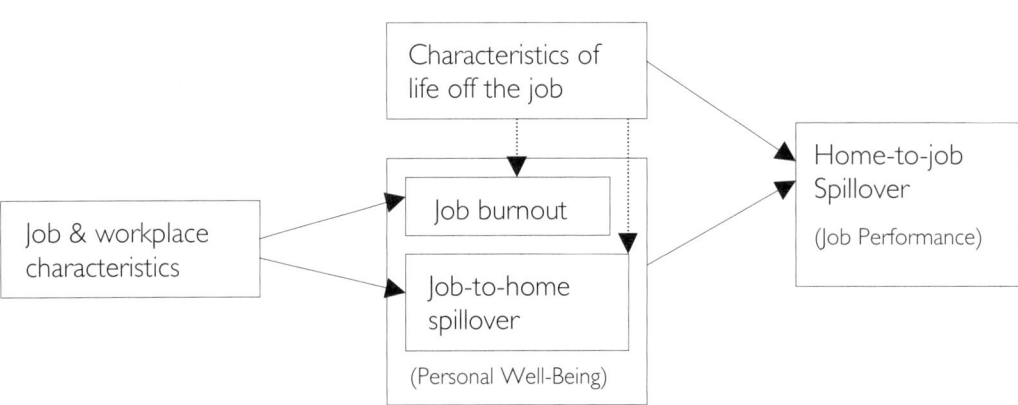

The vertical arrows with dashed lines from characteristics of life off the job to job burnout and job-to-home spillover reflect an additional hypothesis: that some employees may be more susceptible than others to work-related pressures and stress because of various factors in their personal lives. As in the preceding sections, we controlled for basic employee demographics in all analyses prior to evaluating other explanatory factors.

Explaining Job Burnout and Job-to-Home Spillover

Our analyses begin by examining how job and workplace characteristics are related to job burnout and spillover from job to home. Job burnout was measured by asking employees how often they have felt emotionally drained by their jobs, used-up at the end of the workday, stressed out by work, and tired when facing another workday during the past three months. Job-to-home spillover was measured by asking how often in the past three months—*because of their jobs*—employees did not have enough time for themselves, did not have enough time for family or other important people in their lives, did not have the energy to do things with family or others, could not get everything done at home, and were not in as good a mood as they would have liked to have been. (See Chapter 4.) Items were averaged to create job burnout and job-to-home spillover indices for use in data analysis.

Figure 8.6: Job and Workplace Characteristics Explaining Burnout and Job-to-Home Spillover

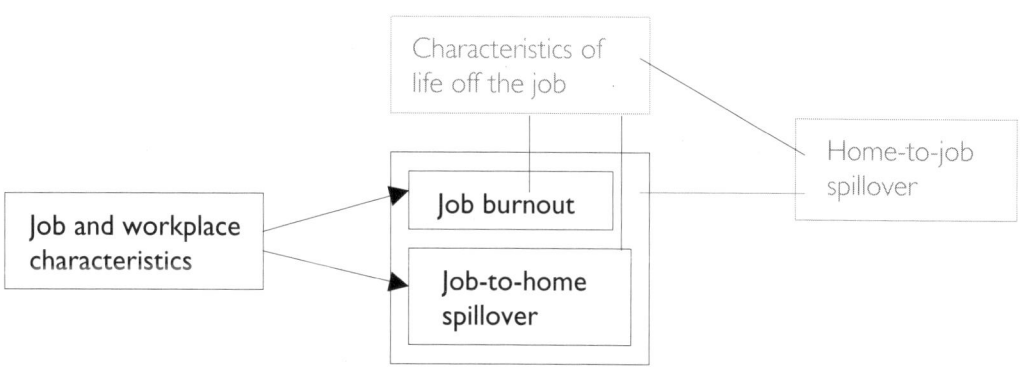

Employee demographics explain 2 percent of the variability in job burnout and 3 percent of the variability in job-to-home spillover, while earnings and access to fringe benefits explain only 1 percent of the variability in each.

Employees with more demanding jobs, poorer-quality jobs, and less supportive workplaces experience greater job burnout than other workers do. Although more supportive workplaces appear to provide a buffer against the negative effects of more demanding jobs, job demands still take a toll.

- Job demands explain 16 percent of the variability in job burnout, with higher demands associated with higher burnout for all job-demand factors, excepting shiftwork, which is unrelated.

- Job quality explains 12 percent of the variability in burnout, with higher job quality associated with lower burnout for all job-quality factors.

- Workplace support explains 19 percent of the variability in burnout, with greater workplace support associated with lower burnout for all factors.

- Together, job demands, job quality, and workplace support explain 33 percent of the variability in burnout.

- To some extent, workplace support appears to buffer or protect employees from the negative effects of job demands, as determined by controlling for workplace factors before evaluating the power of job demands to explain job burnout. However, job demands still account for 11 percent of the variability in burnout after workplace supportiveness is controlled. Job quality does not have any buffering effect.

> Workplace support appears to buffer or protect employees from the negative effects of job demands.

Employees with more demanding jobs, poorer-quality jobs, and less supportive workplaces experience more negative spillover from job to home than others do. Although more supportive workplaces appear to provide a buffer against the negative effects of more demanding jobs, job demands still have considerable negative impact.

- Job demands explain 18 percent of the variability in job-to-home spillover, with higher demands associated with greater job-to-home spillover for all job-demand factors.

- Job quality explains 7 percent of the variability in job-to-home spillover, with higher job quality associated with less job-to-home spillover for all job-quality factors.

- Workplace support explains 14 percent of the variability in job-to-home spillover, with greater workplace support associated with less job-to-home spillover for all factors.

- Together, job demands, job quality, and workplace support explain 29 percent of the variability in job-to-home spillover.

- Workplace support appears to buffer employees somewhat from the negative effects of job demands, as determined by controlling for workplace factors before evaluating the power of job demands to explain job-to-home spillover. However, job demands still account for 14 percent of the variability in job-to-home spillover after workplace supportiveness is controlled. Job quality does not have any buffering effect.

After evaluating the explanatory power of job and workplace characteristics, we evaluated our hypothesis that some workers might be more susceptible than others to feelings of job burnout and negative job-to-home spillover. We did this by determining whether characteristics of life off the job explained any additional variability in job burnout and negative spillover from job to home. Characteristics of employees' lives off the job (Chapter 3) include the following: working multiple jobs; hours worked at job(s) other than main job; commutation time to main job; marital status; parental status (having children under 18 and under 13); living in a dual-earner household or not; frequency of breakdowns in child care arrangements; quality of child care arrangements for children; perceived quality of child care arrangements for respondent; elder care responsibilities in past year and time off work to provide care; current elder care responsibilities and time taken to provide current care; having both child care and elder care responsibilities; amount of time for self on workdays and non-workdays; and total projected household earnings for 1997.

Figure 8.7: Relationships Between Characteristics of Life Off the Job and Job Burnout and Job-to-Home Spillover

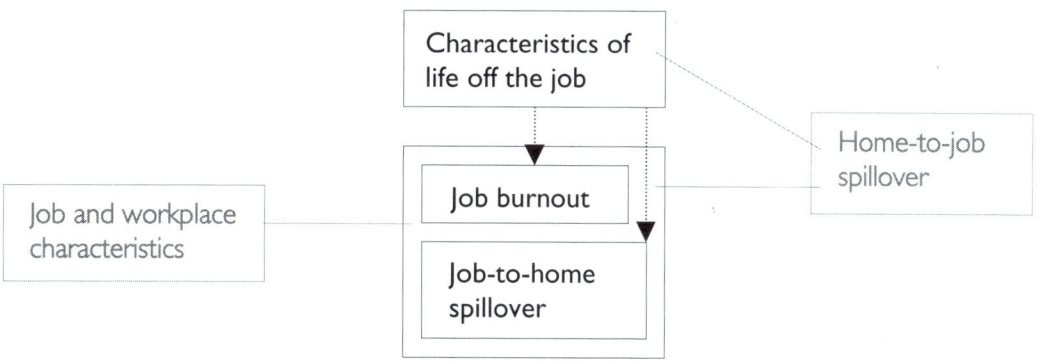

Employees who have lost time from work because of elder care, more often experience breakdowns in their child care arrangements, spend more time commuting to and from work, and have more than one job appear to be slightly more susceptible than others to job burnout.

- Together, characteristics of life off the job explain 2 percent of the variability in job burnout when job and workplace characteristics are held constant. Employees who have lost time from work because of elder care responsibilities, more often experience breakdowns in their regular child care arrangements, spend more time commuting to and from work, and have more than one job appear to be more susceptible than others to job burnout.

> Employees who have children, are married, have less time for themselves away from work, have more than one job, and spend more time commuting also appear to be somewhat more susceptible than others to feelings of negative spillover from their jobs into their personal lives.

- Taken together, off-the-job factors explain 4 percent of the variability in negative spillover from job to home when job and workplace characteristics are held constant. Employees who have less time for themselves off the job,[5] are married, have children, perceive themselves as having poorer-quality child care and more breakdowns in care, spend more time commuting, and have more than one job appear to be more susceptible than others to feelings of negative spillover from their jobs into their personal lives.

> As a group, characteristics of jobs and workplaces explain 33 percent of the variability in job burnout and 29 percent of the variability in job-to-home spillover.

Summary

Both job and workplace factors are strongly related to job burnout and job-to-home spillover, the two linking or mediating factors in the conceptual model described in figure 8.5. As a group, characteristics of jobs and workplaces explain 33 percent of the variability in job burnout and 29 percent of the variability in job-to-home spillover (Figure 8.9).

Although characteristics of employees' lives off the job are not strongly related either to job burnout or to job-to-home spillover, the findings do suggest that some employees are more susceptible than others to feelings of burnout and negative spillover from their jobs, based on differences in family responsibilities, time available for themselves when away from work, perceived quality and reliability of child care arrangements, commutation time, and whether they have multiple jobs.

---

5. The variance in time for self-on workdays and non-workdays associated with work was removed before including these factors in the regression model.

Explaining Home-to-Job Spillover

Following the conceptual model outlined in Figure 8.5 (above), we next examine how characteristics of life off the job, job burnout, and job-to-home spillover are related to spillover from life off the job to work—our indicator of job performance.[6]

Figure 8.8: Explaining Home-to-Job Spillover

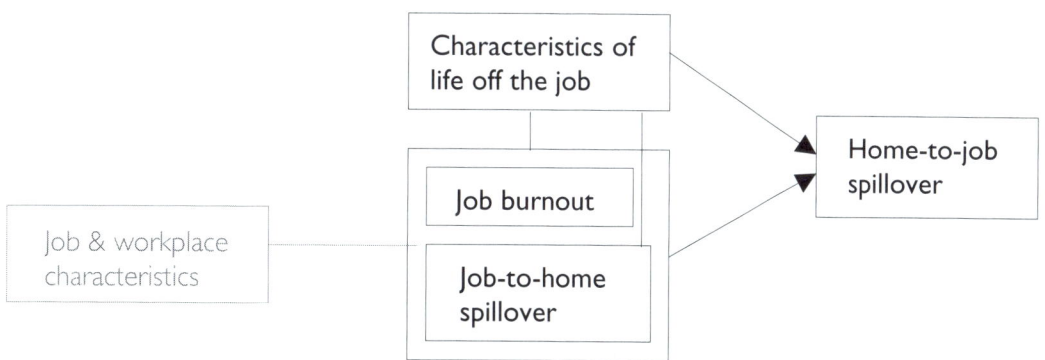

Employee demographics explain only 2 percent of the variability in spillover from life off the job to work.

Characteristics of employees' lives off the job are only modestly related to home-to-job spillover.

- Although life-off-the-job factors were expected to be powerful predictors of spillover from home to job, they only account for 6 percent of the variability in home-to-job spillover. Having children and being dissatisfied with the quality of current child care arrangements are the most powerful independent predictors of negative home-to-job spillover. The next most important factors are having less time for personal activities,[7] losing time from work because of

> Having children and being dissatisfied with the quality of current child care arrangements are the most powerful independent predictors of negative home-to-job spillover.

---

6. Time for self on workdays, time for self on non-workdays, and total projected household earnings for 1997 were regressed on job and workplace variables, and their residuals were incorporated in the analyses summarized here. Household earnings equal respondent's earnings if single, and couple's earnings if married or living with partner.

7. Time available for personal activities was represented as a residual score in the regression model, having first removed the variance explained by job and workplace factors.

elder care responsibilities, and having both child care and elder care responsibilities.

In contrast, employees who experience less job burnout and less negative spillover from job to home also report much less negative spillover from their personal and family lives to their jobs than others do.

- Together, our indices of job burnout and job-to-home spillover explain 18 percent of the variability in spillover from home to job—three times the amount explained by characteristics of life off the job.

The pattern of findings is similar for hourly and salaried employees.

Summary of major findings

Our findings suggest a chain of effects in which excessive job demands lead to job burnout and job spillover that, in turn, lead to spillover from home to work, which diminishes job performance. To some extent, supportive workplaces protect workers from the negative effects of highly demanding jobs, but supportive workplaces are not enough. Job demands and the demands of life off the job both must be manageable for employees to preserve their personal well-being—which ultimately means good mental and physical health—and to be effective workers.

> Job demands and the demands of life off the job both must be manageable for employees to preserve their personal well-being and to be effective workers.

Employers who urge and help employees to achieve a personally satisfying balance may well reap long-term benefits in the form of higher productivity. Moreover, other research suggests that employees' emotional health—measured here by job burnout and job-to-home spillover—is associated with better physical health and lower health care costs overall, another bottom-line concern of business.

Figure 8.9: Home-to-Job Spillover: Relative Explanatory Power

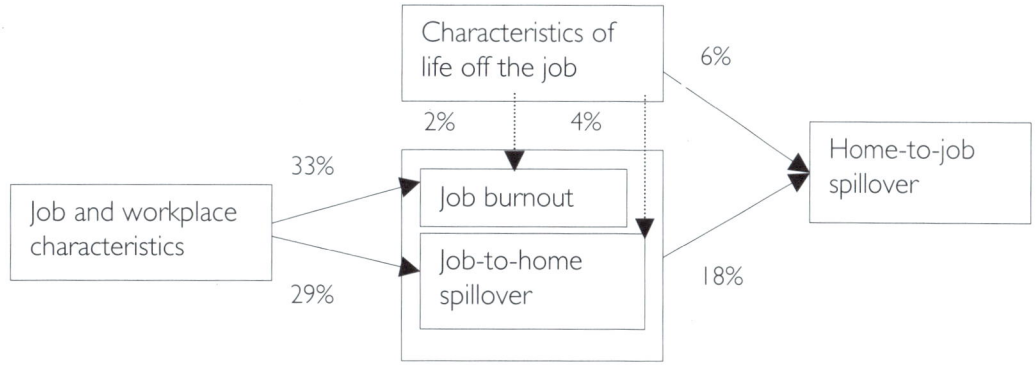

Of course, the benefits of employees' personal well-being flow not only to employers, but also to employees themselves and beyond. Research strongly indicates that better emotional health is associated with more effective parenting, healthier child development, stronger families, better social relations in general, and benefits to communities and society that can be measured both in terms of positive contributions and costs avoided. Thus, we have a potential win-win situation serving the interests of all stakeholders.

The Importance of Pay and Fringe Benefits

One should not conclude from the findings presented in the previous sections that pay, traditional fringe benefits, and dependent-care benefits are of little or no consequence to employees. Rather, it appears that *competitive* pay and fringe benefits are necessary, but not sufficient, conditions for effective recruitment and retention as well as job satisfaction, commitment, loyalty, and productivity.

In preceding sections, we attempted to reach independent conclusions about how pay and benefits are related to many other factors by using descriptive data provided by employees, rather than relying upon employees to make the linkages for us. However, the interview does contain questions about both recruitment and retention that directly ask employees for the reasons they took jobs and why they remain with their current employers. Specifically, employees were asked to provide the main reason they "decided to take a job with their current employer rather than another job" and the main reason they "continue to work for their current employer." Employees' responses to these open-ended questions reflect their perceptions of job markets and personal priorities in ways not captured by other questions in the interview.

When we examine the *main* reasons that employees give for having taken jobs with their current employers,[8] we find that pay is the single most important reason, accounting for 21 percent of responses. Having no other job offers (17 percent) is next most important, followed by a variety of other reasons. Better fringe benefits accounts for 5 percent of responses and more family-friendly policies and benefits for 1 percent. A combination of all reasons that represent job and workplace characteristics considered in previous analyses—except pay and access to benefits—accounts for 39 percent of responses. The overall patterns of response are quite similar for married and single workers, men and women, and parents and non-parents.

> One should not conclude from the findings presented in the previous sections that pay, traditional fringe benefits, and dependent-care benefits are of little or no consequence to employees.

Why do employees stay with their current employers? Again, pay is the single most important reason (25 percent of responses), followed by "more challenging, interesting, stimulating, or fun work" (10 percent) and "more compatible with my personal or family life" (9 percent). Better fringe benefits accounts for 8 percent of responses and more family-friendly policies and benefits for 2 percent. A combination of all reasons that represent job and workplace characteristics considered in previous analyses—except pay and access to benefits—accounts for 46 percent of responses. The overall patterns of response are similar for married and single workers, men and women, and parents and non-parents; however, women are somewhat less likely than men, and non-

---

8. This question was only asked of employees who had worked for their current employer for less than five years.

parents are somewhat less likely than parents, to cite pay as the main reason for continuing with the same employer.

Providing pay that is competitive—relative to what employees could earn elsewhere—is important for successful recruitment and retention. Indeed, if we had asked employees whether they would have taken jobs with their current employers and would remain there even if their pay were not competitive, the importance of pay would undoubtedly be much more pronounced. However, to the extent that *most* employees receive pay that is competitive relative to other jobs they might seek, and equitable within their own workplaces, it is not surprising that for the sample as a whole, *differences* in earnings are un related, or only weakly related, to job satisfaction, commitment, loyalty, and retention.

Regarding access to fringe benefits, findings presented in Chapter 5 reveal that large majorities (74 through 84 percent) of workers have access to traditional fringe benefits—health insurance, retirement plans, paid vacation, paid holidays, and paid sick time—through their jobs. Furthermore, most employees who do not have access to health insurance plans through their jobs, or do not participate in such plans, are covered from other sources. Far fewer employees (11 through 29 percent) have access to dependent-care benefits: child care information and referral services, employer sponsored on- or near-site child care centers, financial assistance for purchasing child care services, dependent care assistance plans, and elder care information and referral services (Chapter 5). The proportions who both have access to these benefits *and* a potential need to utilize them—because they have children under 13 or elder care responsibilities—are smaller still (4 through 11 percent). Because the survey did not collect information about the actual utilization of dependent-care benefits, we cannot examine the relationships between utilization, personal well-being, and employee outcomes on the job.

Although employees are much less likely to select fringe benefits as the main reason for taking or leaving a job, we assume that having the fringe benefits one wants is an important secondary consideration in the decisions of many employees. Nonetheless, to the extent that the benefit packages offered by most employers are competitive within local labor markets and industries, we would not expect *differences* in access to benefits to be strongly related to the employee outcomes examined in this chapter.

> If we had asked employees whether they would have taken jobs with their current employers and would remain there even if their pay were not competitive, the importance of pay would undoubtedly be much more pronounced.

In contrast to pay, traditional fringe benefits, and dependent-care benefits, access to alternative work arrangements is predictive of all employee outcomes. As noted previously, many employers consider at least some flexible work options to be part of their total benefits packages. In our conceptual model, however, we treat flexible work arrangements as characteristics of the workplace environment. Questions in the 1997 survey were not designed to determine whether flexible arrangements are formal policies affecting all workers, normative practices in the workplace, or case-by-case decisions made by supervisors. Unless flexible work options are embodied in formal policies and programs—and they are *not* in many workplaces—we do not think they should be treated as fringe benefits. Flexible work options also differ from traditional fringe benefits and dependent-care benefits in that they typically cannot be translated into direct costs to employers or monetary value to employees. Most important, their effective implementation within an organization depends heavily upon support from the prevailing culture and commitment from managers and supervisors at all levels—very different from having all new hires sign up for a health plan or providing an 800 number for child care referrals. As a result, employees' access to flexible work arrangements seems likely to vary more than their access to traditional fringe benefits and dependent-care benefits—both *across* and *within* organizations—and to be more strongly related to individual outcomes.

A final caveat: Data from the survey do not allow us to identify employees who work for organizations—typically large corporations—that have developed integrated initiatives to address the needs of workers both on and off the job. Such initiatives—often referred to as work-life programs—seek to more systematically and comprehensively respond to employees' needs by coordinating traditional fringe benefits, dependent-care benefits, alternative work options, employee assistance programs, wellness programs, and so forth. Increasingly, such programs receive support from the highest levels of management and may be separately staffed. The most sophisticated of these programs are also very proactive, seeking to affect the behavior of managers and supervisors at all levels in order to change the social climate and culture of the workplace and even the characteristics of jobs. Whether or not such initiatives are successful in improving recruitment, productivity, and retention, as well as having a positive impact on the well-being of employees and their families, cannot be determined by this study. However, our findings do suggest that they may well be on the right track.

9 Current and Emerging Issues

In this chapter, we consider three crosscutting issues that either have attracted or will attract public and business attention. First, we evaluate various stereotypes applied to Generation X to determine whether and to what extent Gen Xers really differ from other workers. Second, we examine the current prevalence and impact of elder care on the wage and salaried labor force and explore the implications of growing elder care needs for both employees and employers. Third, we investigate whether there is a backlash among young, unmarried, and childless workers against work-family benefits and against having to accommodate the personal and family needs of coworkers.

Generation X

Broad negative generalizations about Generation X are not supported by the findings presented here. "Gen Xers" are very much like Baby Boomers were at the same age and not much different from boomers today. A moderate amount of job-hopping has characterized young workers for at least the past two decades. The best apparent antidote to high turnover among Gen-X employees is to provide them with high-quality jobs and supportive workplaces—the same things that older workers want.

Members of Generation X (young workers 18 through 32 years old in 1997) have often been portrayed in the popular press as nonconformists with an aversion to hard work who hop from job to job with little concern for their employers. At the same time, employers depend increasingly on the labor of Gen Xers in an era of very tight labor markets and seek more effective ways to recruit and retain them. Does Generation X differ from the preceding generation of young workers? Has there been a cultural shift in work ethic and work habits? How do Gen Xers and Baby Boomers compare today?

The analyses presented in this section of the report rely heavily upon comparisons between young workers 18 through 32 years old in 1997 and workers who were 18 through 32 in 1977. Interestingly, today's Baby Boomers, a major source of complaints about Generation X, made up most of the workforce under 33 years old in 1977. For purposes of comparing 1997 and 1977, the 1997 National Study of the Changing Workforce (NCSW) sample was restricted, to parallel the sample selected for the 1977 Quality of Employment Survey (QES) study[9]. When occasional comparisons are made between Generation X and older employees in 1997, the full 1997 sample is similarly restricted to employees working 20 or more hours per week.

Generation X makes up a significantly smaller proportion of the U.S. labor force than their age peers in 1977 did.

- While workers from 18 through 32 years of age represented 44 percent of the wage and salaried labor force in 1977, their proportion of the labor force is only 29 percent in 1997. The current labor force is dominated by an exceptionally large number of postwar baby-boom cohorts, now 33 through 51 years of age, who are in their prime years of employment.

Members of Generation X are much better educated, as well as more racially and ethnically diverse, than their age peers 20 years ago were.

- In 1997, 64 percent of workers 18 through 32 years old have some education beyond high school, whereas in 1977 only 44 percent did—a difference of 20 percentage points.

- Twice as many Gen Xers belong to ethnic and racial minority groups—24 percent in 1997—as their age peers two decades ago did—12 percent.

These trends toward more education and greater diversity in the workforce have been widely noted and promise to continue.

Members of Generation X are less likely to be legally married than their age peers in 1977 were, but they are just as likely to live in marriage like relationships with either spouses or partners.

- Gen-X employees are less likely (40 percent) to be legally married than employees of comparable ages in 1977 (52 percent) were. However, the same proportions of Gen Xers and their age peers from 1977 (52 percent) live in marriage-like relationships with either spouses or partners.

- The proportion of young workers 18 through 32 years of age living with partners outside marriage has increased by a substantial 12 percentage points over the past 20 years. In all likelihood, employers are unaware of just how many officially "single" young workers have

> In all likelihood, employers are unaware of just how many officially "single" young workers have family lives like those of their formally married peers.

---

9. The main difference between screening criteria for the 1997 and 1977 surveys was hours worked per week, with the 1997 National Study of the Changing Workforce sample including all persons engaged in paid work for any number of hours per week, and the 1977 Quality of Employment Survey including only persons working 20 or more hours per week. Two other minor differences in sample screening criteria were also accounted for by restricting the 1977 sample to workers 18 or older and restricting the 1997 sample to respondents interviewed in English. These restrictions reduced the 1997 sample by 152 cases and the 1977 sample by 15 cases.

family lives like those of their formally married peers and do or could benefit from family-friendly benefits, programs, and policies in the workplace that include partners as well as spouses.

Young workers today are just as likely to have children as young workers 20 years ago were.

- The proportion of employees 18 through 32 years who are parents is the same for 1997 and 1977: 41 percent have children under 18, 39 percent have children under 13, and 31 percent have children under 6 years old in their households.

Married Gen Xers—with and without children—are more likely to have an employed spouse than young workers in 1977 were, and both members of employed couples are more likely to work full-time.

- In 1997, 82 percent of married Gen Xers live in dual-earner households, compared with 69 percent of married workers 18 through 32 in 1977.

- The discrepancy between 1997 and 1977 is even larger for young married workers with children under 18. Among married employees with children, 75 percent of Gen Xers have employed spouses, compared with 61 percent of their age peers in 1977. (Figure 9.1)

Because a smaller proportion of Baby Boomers lived in dual-earner households when they were young marrieds, substantial numbers of Boomers may not empathize with the stresses and strains Gen Xers experience in dual-earner households.

Figure 9.1: Married Couples with Children Living in Dual- and Single-Earner Families

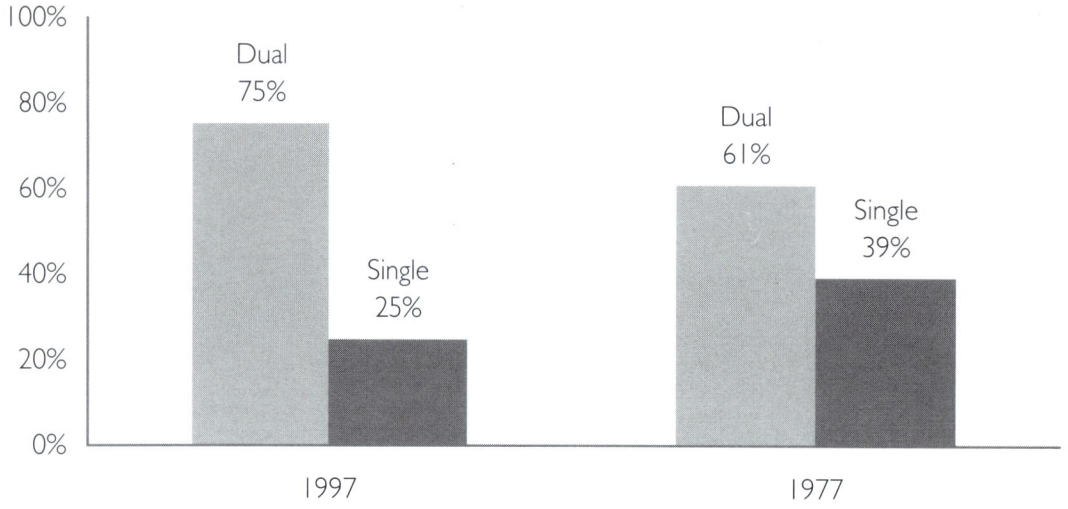

In concert with women's increasing labor-force participation, the attitudes of young workers toward working wives and mothers have become much more favorable over the past two decades.

- Whereas 36 percent of Generation X feel "it is much better for everyone involved if the man earns the money and the woman takes care of the home and children," 56 percent of young workers 20 years ago felt that way.

- Interestingly, today's Boomers, who were those young workers 20 years ago, are still somewhat more likely (41 percent) than Generation X to feel that it is better for women to stay at home, though over time they have become more accepting of women in the labor force.

Contrary to the portrayal of Generation X in popular media, young workers today are not a group of "slackers." They work substantially longer hours and find their jobs more demanding than young workers 20 years ago did.

- Hours are long today. On average, Gen Xers work 45 total hours a week at their main jobs and 47 hours a week at all of their jobs combined. In contrast, young workers 20 years ago averaged 41 total hours a week at their main jobs and 43 hours at all of their jobs combined.

- Particularly striking is the finding that 62 percent of Gen Xers work more than 40 hours a week, including both paid and unpaid time, at their primary jobs, compared with 37 percent of young workers in 1977.

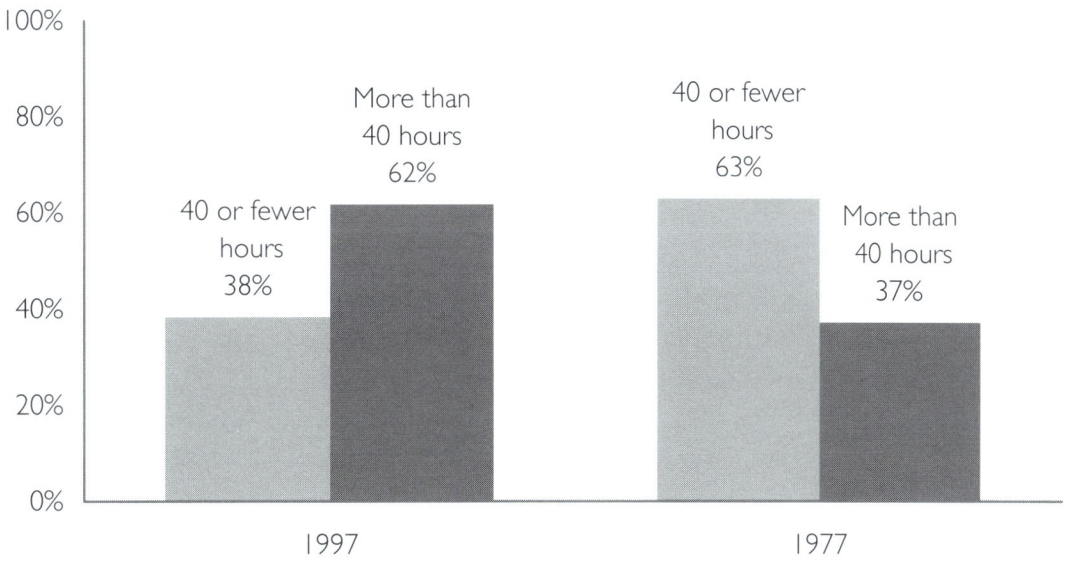

Figure 9.2: Comparison of All Hours Worked Per Week at Primary Jobs by Workers 18 - 32 Years Old in 1997 and 1977

- Young workers today also perceive their jobs as more demanding than young workers in 1977 did. Specifically, Gen Xers report working harder and faster and not having enough time to get everything done.

Members of Generation X feel somewhat more satisfied with their jobs but perceive less job security than young workers 20 years ago did.

- Ninety percent of Gen Xers feel generally satisfied with their jobs, compared with 82 percent of their age peers in 1977.

- More than one quarter (27 percent) of young workers in 1997 feel it is very or somewhat likely they will lose their jobs within the next two years—a substantial increase from the 15 percent reported 20 years earlier.

> 62 percent of Gen Xers work more than 40 hours a week, including both paid and unpaid time, at their primary jobs, compared with 37 percent of young workers in 1977.

Generation-X employees are less likely than Baby Boomers were to have embarked upon their work lives imagining they would remain with the same company for most of their careers. However, half of all Gen Xers and Boomers now view expectations of a lifetime job as passé.

Because this question was not asked in 1977, comparisons with the responses of young workers 20 years ago are not possible. However, baby-boomer employees in 1997 were asked to reflect on the time when they entered the labor force, which provides a retrospective point of comparison for the analysis reported here. Only employees working 20 or more hours per week are included in the analytic sample.

- Gen Xers are less likely (41 percent) than Baby Boomers (54 percent) to report that when they first started working, they imagined they would spend their working lives mainly with one company or organization.

- Fifty-one percent of today's Gen Xers and Baby Boomers believe that in today's world, workers should not expect any company to provide a lifetime job. Yet, an almost equal proportion feel that employers do have a responsibility to provide job security.

> Fifty-one percent of today's Gen Xers and Baby Boomers believe that in today's world, workers should not expect any company to provide a lifetime job.

Though most Gen Xers do not expect to stay in the same jobs forever, they are not a generation of job-hoppers. Moreover, they feel just as loyal to their employers, and say that they are just as willing to work harder than required for the success of their companies, as older workers are.

- Overall, 22 percent of young workers in both 1997 and 1977 said it was very likely they would make a genuine effort to find a new job with another employer in the coming year, while 53 percent in both years said it was not at all likely they would do so.

- Comparing workers under 33 years old with workers 33 and older in both years, however, does reveal that in 1977 younger workers were, and in 1997 are, more likely than older workers to be planning a job change. Young workers, of course, are still exploring job opportunities and developing occupational paths, which naturally leads them to try out different jobs with different employers during their early years in the labor force.

- Findings from the survey provide no evidence that members of Generation X are less committed to their employers than older workers are, as measured by expressed loyalty and willingness to work harder than they have to in order to help their companies succeed.

For Generation X, as for employees in general, retention is most strongly associated with having better-quality jobs and more supportive workplaces.

The relationships between probable retention of younger employees for at least one year and employee demographics, job characteristics, and workplace characteristics were examined by applying the conceptual model presented in Chapter 1 and the data analysis methods used in Chapter 8. To parallel other analyses in this section, the 1997 sample was restricted to employees working 20 or more hours per week and interviewed in English. All analyses of job and workplace factors controlled for employee demographics, which explain 5 percent of the variability in retention.

- As a group, earnings and traditional benefits (Chapter 5) explain only 4 percent of the variability in probable retention for at least one year. Earnings are not independently related to retention. However, workers with more generous traditional benefits and access to more generous dependent care benefits are somewhat more likely to envision staying with their current employer for at least the next year.

- As a group, job demands (Chapter 5) explain only 4 percent of the variability in retention. Only two of six variables in the job-demands group are independently related to retention. Generation X employees required to work paid or unpaid overtime with little or no notice are more likely to say they plan to make a genuine effort to find a new job with another employer in the coming year, and those who perceive their jobs as more demanding are slightly more likely to be planning a move.

- Job quality, a group of five factors, explains 13 percent of the variability in retention, far more than earnings, benefits, and job demands explain. All five factors are independently related to retention. Younger employees with more job autonomy, learning opportunities, meaningful jobs, job security, and personal opportunity for advancement are more likely to plan on staying with their current employers for at least the next year.

- The importance of workplace supportiveness as a predictor of retention parallels that of job quality. The seven factors in the workplace support group explain 11 percent of the variability in retention, and all factors are independently related to retention. Like other employees, Gen Xers who work in environments that are flexible, supportive, respectful, fair, and responsive to their individual needs—as persons with lives off the job—are more likely to plan on staying with their current employers for at least the next year.

> Like other employees, Gen Xers who work in environments that are flexible, supportive, respectful, fair, and responsive to their individual needs—as persons with lives off the job—are more likely to plan on staying with their current employers for at least the next year.

Implications

Our research does not support negative stereotypes of Generation X. We find no massive shift in work ethic or behavior over the past 20 years. What we do find is that members of Generation X are working harder and more often coping with the stresses of dual-earner family life than Baby Boomers did when they were the same age.

As for employers' concerns about retaining Gen-X employees, who are in short supply, our findings again suggest that higher job quality and workplace support that is responsive to basic individual needs both on and off the job are the factors most likely to increase retention—assuming that wages and fringe benefits are competitive.

Elder Care

The survey reveals that one out of four wage and salaried workers in the U.S. labor force had elder care responsibilities during the past year. Moreover, of workers who provided elder care, more than one-third lost time from work to do so. As the U.S. population continues to age, growing elder care responsibilities promise to have an even greater impact on the workforce.

Historically, and still today, families provide the major part of non-medical care for elderly relatives. As the population ages and labor-force participation expands, however, the supply of non-employed family members available to provide care is not keeping pace with needs. Looking into the future, one sees that elder care will demand time and attention from growing numbers of employees, affecting the way they work.

In the 1997 survey, elder care is defined as providing "special attention to or care for someone 65 years old or older."

The population of the United States is aging, and responsibilities for elder care affect growing numbers of workers and employers.

- While only 13 percent of workers had elder care responsibilities when interviewed, 25 percent—a quarter of the U.S. wage and salaried labor force—had had such responsibilities during the preceding year. (Figure 9.3)

- Fully 42 percent of the U.S. workforce expects to provide elder care within the next 5 years.

While older workers are more likely to have elder care responsibilities, surprising numbers of younger workers do too.

- Older workers are much more likely to have had elder care responsibilities in the past year—37 percent of workers 50 and over versus 28 percent of workers 40 to 49, 19 percent of workers 30 to 39, and 18 percent of workers under 30. Although elder care is certainly concentrated among older employees, surprisingly large proportions of younger workers— nearly one fifth of "thirty-" and even "twenty-somethings"—also have elder care responsibilities over the course of a year.

> Although elder care is certainly concentrated among older employees, surprisingly large proportions of younger workers also have elder care responsibilities over the course of a year.

Figure 9.3: Prevalence of Elder Care in the U.S. Labor Force

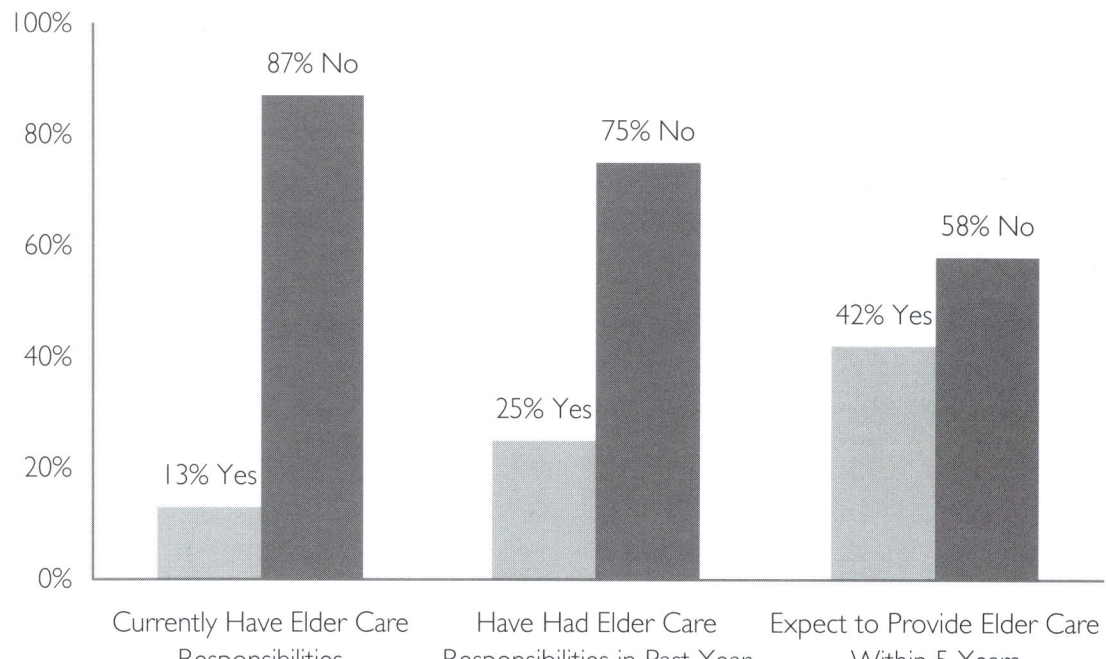

The proportions of working men and women with elder care responsibilities are virtually the same.

- Women are slightly more likely (27 percent) to have had elder care responsibilities over the past year than men (23 percent). Among employees providing elder care in the past year, 48 percent are men and 52 percent women. There are no differences between men and women in "current" or projected "future" responsibilities.

Nearly one in 10 employees and one in five working parents has been part of the so-called "sandwich generation" during the past year.

- Twenty percent of employed parents—representing nine percent of all employees—have had both child care and elder care responsibilities at some time in the past year.

Employees with elder care responsibilities spend an average of nearly eleven hours per week providing assistance, with men and women spending equal amounts of time.

- An average of 7.5 hours per week (median of 5 hours) is devoted to personal care—meal preparation, physical care, housework, transportation, and so on—while a mean of 3.3 hours (median of 2 hours) is spent on other types of assistance—arranging services, making appointments, checking in by phone to make sure everything is all right, handling finances, and so forth. This represents an average of eleven hours and a median of 8.3 hours of care of all types. For some workers the hours devoted to care are much higher.

- Although earlier research, including our own 1992 survey, has sometimes found that employed women spend more time on elder care than employed men do, data from the 1997 survey do not confirm this finding. Based on self-reports, at least, men and women appear to devote equal time to personal and other types of assistance for elders in their care.

> Men and women appear to devote equal time to personal and other types of assistance for elders in their care.

Elder care frequently takes time away from work.

- Among workers who had elder care responsibilities in the past year, more than one third reduced their work hours or took time off to provide that care, while 63 percent did not.

Figure 9.4: Took Time Off Work or Reduced Work Hours During Past Year Because of Elder Care Responsibilities

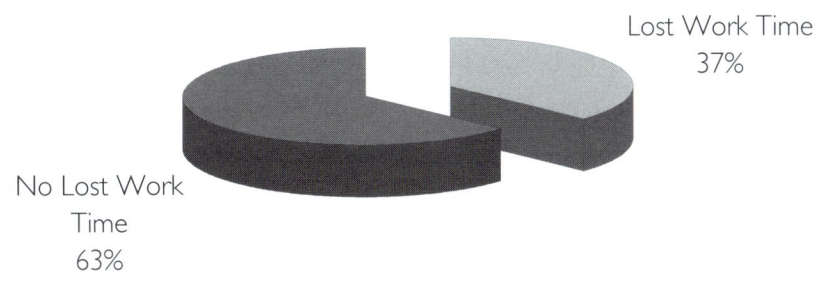

Lost Work Time 37%

No Lost Work Time 63%

- Employees with higher personal earnings are more likely to reduce their work hours or take time off than workers with lower earnings, suggesting that more highly paid employees may be better able to both negotiate time off and afford it.

Surprisingly, employed men with elder care responsibilities in the past year were just as likely as employed women to have taken time off or reduced their work hours to provide care.

- Among employees with elder care responsibilities, there was no difference between men and women in the proportion who took time off or reduced their work hours—37 percent overall.

Many employers appear to be at least informally supportive of workers who take time off or reduce work hours to provide elder care. However, more advantaged employees are more able to take as much time as they need without losing pay.

- Of the 37 percent of employees who took time off or reduced their work schedules during the past year to meet elder care responsibilities, 91 percent feel their employers were somewhat or very helpful, and 63 percent were able to take as much time away from work as they needed without losing pay.

- Personal earnings, household income, and occupational status are not related to ratings of employer helpfulness. However, employees with higher earnings and employees in managerial and professional occupations are more able than other workers to take as much time off as they needed without losing pay.

Only one in four employees has access to elder care resource and referral services through his or her employer.

- Only 25 percent of workers have access to elder care resource and referral services through their employers—services that can provide crucial emotional support, practical guidance, and access to community services for employees confronted with major elder care responsibilities.

- Managers, professionals, and higher-paid employees in general are more likely than other workers to report that their employers offer elder care resource and referral services.

> Employees with higher earnings and employees in managerial and professional occupations are more able than other workers to take as much time off as they need to provide elder care without losing pay.

Implications

With today's smaller families, single-parent families, and two-career couples, the pool of able-bodied, non-employed adults available to provide elder care is shrinking just as demand for care is rising. It is not clear that anyone—employees, employers, community agencies, or government—is prepared for the substantial impact that growing elder care responsibilities will have on the labor force in coming years. Although no one expects employers to address the full range of issues raised by this demographic tidal wave, employers who do not anticipate the potential disruptions to their workforces will likely be taken aback by the consequences.

Work-Family Backlash

Despite claims in the press and worries in the boardroom, we found no evidence that young, unmarried, or childless employees are more likely than other workers to resent work-family benefits that do not benefit them personally. Nor are they more likely to resent doing extra work occasionally to accommodate coworkers' family or personal needs.

In general, the demographic characteristics of individual workers bear little relationship to either their acceptance of work-family benefits that are not personally beneficial to them or their willingness to do extra work to accommodate the personal and family needs of coworkers. Rather, characteristics of the workplace—flexibility, supportive supervisors, good coworker relations, and supportive workplace cultures—relate most strongly and positively to employees' acceptance of work-family benefits and willingness to accommodate coworkers' needs.

Attitudes Toward Work-Family Benefits Provided by Employers

After more than a decade of systematic effort by many employers to help employees more effectively balance work with their lives off the job, some have begun to ask themselves whether they have gone too far. A recent spate of media reports and even a television sitcom have purported to give voice to the resentment of young, unmarried, and childless workers who believe that coworkers with families are being given special treatment.

It is worth remembering from Chapter 3 that fully 85 percent of employees live with family members of one sort or another. Thus, to the extent that work-family benefits extend to grandchildren in one's custody, adopted and foster children, unmarried partners, parents, and other relatives, such benefits should be relevant to the vast majority of the wage and salaried labor force. Family members who don't reside with employees may also benefit, as is the case with long-term care insurance plans that allow participation by employees' parents. Moreover, even when work-family benefits are not immediately useful, they might have been so at an earlier stage—or may still be at a later stage—in an employee's life. Such circumstances provide a backdrop for interpreting the findings presented in this section.

> To the extent that work-family benefits extend to grandchildren in one's custody, adopted and foster children, unmarried partners, parents, and other relatives, such benefits should be relevant to the vast majority of the wage and salaried labor force.

Six in 10 employees say they would not resent their employers' providing work-family benefits that did not benefit them personally. This proportion has remained constant since 1992.

- Sixty percent of workers indicate they would not be resentful if their employers provided work-family benefits that were not personally beneficial to them, while 40 percent would be resentful. (Twenty-two percent agreed strongly that they would be resentful, while 37 percent disagreed strongly.)

- The proportion of workers (about 40 percent) who would resent their employers' offering work-family benefits that are not personally beneficial to them has neither increased nor decreased over the past five years, despite the expansion of work-family and work-life programs.[10]

- Although resentment did not increase from 1992 to 1997, the extent of resentment within the workforce is substantial enough that employers should try to understand and be aware of it as they develop, communicate, and implement new programs.

Contrary to popular opinion, young, unmarried, or childless employees are not more likely than other workers to say they would resent work-family benefits that do not benefit them personally.

- No differences were found by age, comparing workers from Generation X with members of the baby-boom generation and so-called mature workers 52 and older; by marital status; or by parental status (children under 18 living at home). (Figures 9.5 and 9.6)

> The proportion of workers who would resent their employers' offering work-family benefits that are not personally beneficial to them has neither increased nor decreased over the past five years, despite the expansion of work-family and work-life programs.

---

10. Four-level responses ranging from strongly agree to strongly disagree were dichotomized to simplify the comparison of 1997 with 1992 data and reduce bias that might be introduced by difference in the labeling of intermediate response categories (agree vs. somewhat agree; disagree vs. somewhat disagree).

Figure 9.5: Percentage of Employees Who Would Resent Work Family Benefits That Are Not Personally Beneficial—By Age

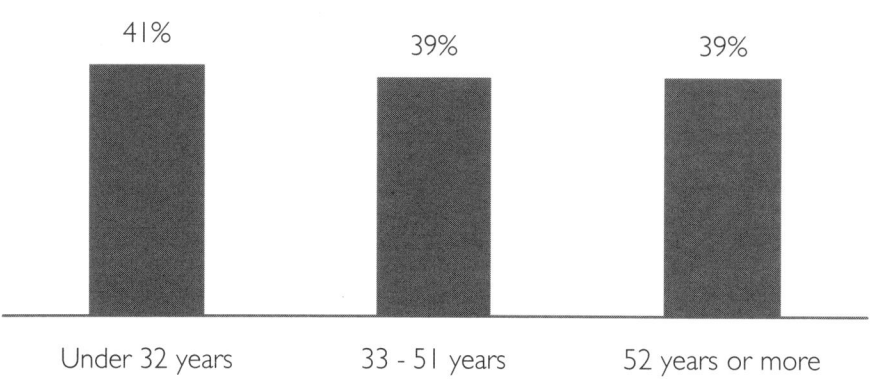

Resentment by Age

Under 32 years	33 - 51 years	52 years or more
41%	39%	39%

Figure 9.6: Percentage of Employees Who Would Resent Work-Family Benefits That Are Not Personally Beneficial—By Parental and Marital Status

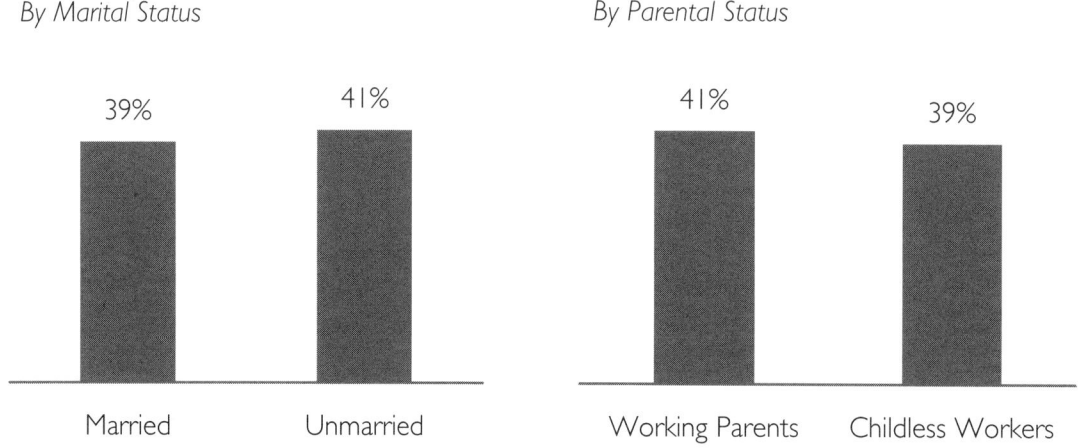

By Marital Status

Married	Unmarried
39%	41%

By Parental Status

Working Parents	Childless Workers
41%	39%

So who is resentful?

To address this question we applied the conceptual model presented in Chapter 1 and conducted analyses paralleling those in Chapter 8. Employee demographics are examined first, then controlled for in subsequent analyses.[11]

Employees who have less education, have non-managerial or non-professional jobs, and classify themselves as belonging to a racial or ethnic minority group are more likely than others to say they would resent benefits that do not help them personally.

Taken together, employee demographics explain 6 percent of the variability in resentment. Of the six factors in this group (Chapter 2), only education, occupation, and minority status are related to resentment. It may also be helpful to note here that employees with higher household earnings—considered later in this section as a characteristic of life off the job—would also be less resentful than other workers of work-family benefits that do not benefit them personally. Do less advantaged employees fear they may become even more disadvantaged if the benefits piece of the total compensation pie serves others more than them? Have better educated workers developed attitudes and values more accepting of work-family benefits that serve changing life-cycle needs? Do cultural differences not measured in the survey account for differences between the racial/ethnic majority and various minorities included in the sample? Given the available information, we can only speculate about the answers to such questions.

Employees' earnings and access to fringe benefits are not related to resentment, nor are characteristics of their lives off the job.

Characteristics of life off the job are described in Chapter 3; benefits, in Chapter 5.

- Having access to more or less generous traditional fringe benefits (health insurance, pension and retirement plans, paid vacation, and so on) or dependent-care benefits (child care services, child care subsidies, child care resource and referral, and so on) is not related to resentment. This finding lends no support to speculation that employees with access to fewer traditional benefits and/or more dependent-care benefits not directly beneficial to them would be more resentful than other workers of work-family benefits offered by their employers.

- As a group, characteristics of life off the job are not significantly related to resentment. Indeed, only one of 19 factors has any independent relationship to resentment. Employees

---

11. After controlling for employee demographics, the contribution of each group or block of independent variables considered in this section was tested independently. Statements about the independent contributions of individual independent variables are based on partial correlations with the dependent variable prior to their inclusion in the regression equation.

with higher household incomes are slightly less likely than other workers to say they would resent work-family benefits that are not personally beneficial to them.

Job demands and job quality are only weakly related to resentment.

The six factors labeled *job demands* and the five factors labeled *job quality* are described in Chapter 5.

- As a group, job-demand factors explain only 1 percent of the variability in resentment toward work-family benefits, with only one of six factors being independently and weakly associated with higher resentment.

- As a group, job-quality factors explain only 1 percent of the variability in resentment, with high quality on three of five factors being independently and weakly associated with lower resentment.

And who is least resentful?

Employees whose workplaces are more flexible and supportive are less likely than employees in less supportive workplaces to say they would resent work-family benefits that are not personally beneficial to them. This finding suggests that employers who create genuinely family-friendly work climates and cultures may actually experience less backlash than others.

The seven factors labeled *workplace support* are described in Chapter 6.

- As a group, workplace-support factors explain 5 percent of the variability in resentment. Employees in more supportive workplaces—as measured by flexibility, supervisor supportiveness, supportive workplace culture, and supportive coworkers—are less likely to be resentful than workers in less supportive workplaces.

Employees working in more responsive and supportive environments may be more accepting of benefits that do not benefit them personally, at the moment, because they have come to understand the changing life-cycle needs served by work-family benefits that their coworkers use and that they themselves have used in the past or may use in the future.

> Employees in more supportive workplaces are less likely to be resentful than workers in less supportive workplaces.

160 *Current and Emerging Issues*

Attitudes Toward Accommodating Coworkers With Personal and Family Needs

The press has also reported that young, unmarried, and childless workers increasingly resent having to do extra work because of working parents who take time off for sick children, school closings, maternity leave, paternity leave, soccer games, teachers meetings, and so on. But just how widespread is such resentment?

Relatively few workers say they would resent having to do extra work occasionally to accommodate the personal or family needs of coworkers, and the proportion has not grown since 1992.

- Only 16.5 percent of workers say they would resent having to do extra work occasionally to accommodate the personal or family needs of coworkers, while 83.5 percent would not be resentful. (Only 6 percent agreed strongly that they would be resentful, while 54 percent disagreed strongly.) (Figure 9.7)

- Resentment of having to do extra work occasionally to accommodate coworkers' personal and family needs has neither increased nor decreased over the past five years, remaining steady at 16.5 percent of the wage and salaried labor force.[12]

> Only 16½ percent of workers say they would resent having to do extra work occasionally to accommodate the personal or family needs of coworkers.

---

12. Four-level responses ranging from strongly agree to strongly disagree were dichotomized to simplify the comparison of 1997 with 1992 data and reduce bias that might be introduced by differences in the labeling of intermediate response categories in the two years (agree vs. somewhat agree; disagree vs. somewhat disagree).

Figure 9.7: Would Resent Having to Do Extra Work Occasionally to Accommodate Co-Workers' Personal/Family Needs?

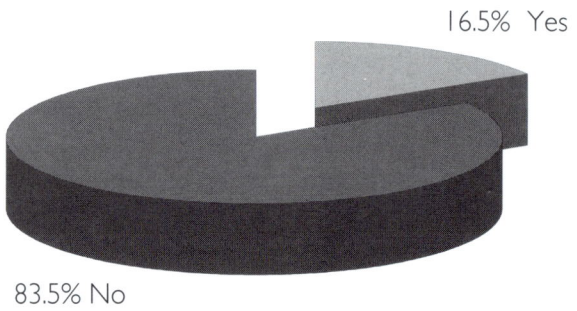

16.5% Yes

83.5% No

Young, unmarried, or childless workers are no more likely than others to say they would resent doing extra work occasionally to accommodate the personal and family needs of coworkers.

- As was the case with work-family benefits, no differences in resentment were found by age, comparing workers from Generation X with members of the baby-boom generation and so-called mature workers 52 and older; by marital status; or by parental status (children under 18 at home).

Then which workers are resentful?

To address this question we again applied the conceptual model presented in Chapter 1 and conducted analyses paralleling those in Chapter 8. Employee demographics are examined first, then controlled for in subsequent analyses.

Male employees, employees who have less education, and employees who belong to racial or ethnic minority groups are slightly more likely than others to say they would resent having to do extra work to accommodate coworkers' personal and family needs.

Taken together, employee demographics (described in Chapter 2) explain less than 2 percent of the variability in resentment of having to do extra work to accommodate coworkers. Only three of six factors in the employee-demographics group are at all related to resentment—gender, education, and minority status. Questions similar to those raised regarding the underlying causes of the relationships between demographics and resentment toward work-family benefits could also be raised here, but when all is said and done, the survey data severely limited further exploration of possible answers.

Employees' earnings and access to fringe benefits are not related to resentment of having to do extra work to accommodate the personal and family needs of coworkers, nor are characteristics of their lives off the job.

Characteristics of life off the job are described in Chapter 3; benefits, in Chapter 5.

- Having access to more or less generous traditional fringe benefits (health insurance, pension and retirement plans, paid vacation, and so forth) or dependent-care benefits (child care services, child care subsidies, child care resource and referral, and so on) is not related to resentment.

- As a group, characteristics of life off the job are not significantly related to resentment. Indeed, only one of 19 factors has any independent relationship to resentment. Employees who live in dual-earner households are slightly less likely to say they would resent doing extra work to help coworkers.

Job demands and job quality are only weakly related to resentment.

The six factors labeled *job demands* and the five factors labeled *job quality* are described in Chapter 5.

- As a group, job-demand factors explain only 1 percent of the variability in resentment of having to do extra work to accommodate coworkers, with only one of six factors being independently and weakly associated with higher resentment.

- As a group, job-quality factors explain only 1 percent of the variability in resentment. However, all five job-quality factors were independently, albeit weakly, associated with lower resentment.

And who is least resentful?

By far the most important factors accounting for resentment of having to do extra work to help coworkers are inherent in the workplace and not in workers themselves. Employees whose workplaces are more supportive with respect to flexibility, supervisors, coworkers, and the general culture are less likely to resent having to do extra work occasionally to accommodate the personal and family needs of coworkers than workers in less supportive workplaces.

The seven factors labeled *workplace support* are described in Chapter 6.

- As a group, workplace-support factors explain 12 percent of the variability in resentment. Employees in more supportive workplaces—as measured by flexibility, supervisor supportiveness, supportive workplace culture, supportive coworkers, lack of discrimination, and respect—are less likely to be resentful than workers in less supportive workplaces.

Implications

It would appear that employers who have made greater progress in creating person- and family-friendly work environments actually experience less work-family backlash. To a large extent, supportive workplace factors are within the control of employers to alter, unlike the personal demographic characteristics that workers bring to the job. However, creating a highly supportive workplace environment is more challenging than simply implementing another discrete benefit or program from the top down. Indeed, for many employers, it requires fundamental changes in workplace culture and social climate.

> Creating a highly supportive workplace environment is more challenging than simply implementing another discrete benefit or program from the top down. Indeed, for many employers, it requires fundamental changes in workplace culture and social climate.

Technical Appendix

This report focuses on findings from the Family and Work Institute's 1997 National Study of the Changing Workforce (NSCW). However, we also compare data from the 1997 survey with data from two other sources—our 1992 NSCW survey and the 1977 Quality of Employment Survey (QES). All three surveys included both self-employed and wage and salaried workers in the U.S. labor force; however, only wage and salaried workers are included in the samples analyzed for this report. Each of the three surveys is described briefly here.

1997 National Study of The Changing Workforce

The 1997 NSCW survey was conducted by Louis Harris and Associates using a questionnaire developed by the Families and Work Institute. A total of 3,551 interviews were completed with a nationwide cross-section of employed adults between March 14 and July 27, 1997. Interviews, which averaged 40 minutes in length, were conducted by telephone using a computer-assisted telephone interviewing (CATI) system. Calls were made to a stratified unclustered random probability sample generated by random-digit-dial methods. Up to 20 calls were made per telephone number to determine eligibility and, if appropriate, to complete interviews. Interviewers coded open-ended responses, with the exception of those concerning occupation and industry, which were coded by the U.S. Bureau of the Census using current three-digit classifications.

Sample eligibility was limited to people who 1) worked at a paid job or operated an income-producing business, 2) were 18 years or older, 3) were in the civilian labor force, 4) resided in the contiguous 48 states, and 5) lived in a noninstitutional residence—that is, a household—with a telephone. In households with more than one eligible person, one was randomly selected to be interviewed. Interviewers offered cash honoraria of $20 as incentives.

Of the total 19,057 telephone numbers called, 8,149 were found to be nonresidential or nonworking numbers, and 2,338 were determined to be ineligible residences. Of the remaining telephone numbers, 3,739 were determined to represent eligible households, and interviews were completed for 3,551 of these—*a completion rate of 95 percent*. However, eligibility or ineligibility could not be determined in the remaining 4,831 cases.

Among those contacts for which eligibility could be determined, the eligibility ratio was 61.5 [3,739/(3,739+2,338)]. Thus, we estimate that 61.5 percent of the 4,831 cases for which eligibility could not be determined—2,971 cases in all—might have been eligible households. Dividing the number of completed interviews (3,551) by the number of known eligibles (3,739) plus the number of estimated eligibles (2,971) yields an *overall response rate of 52.9 percent for potentially eligible households.*

The sample was first weighted by the number of eligibles in the respondents' households, then to proportions in the March 1996 Current Population Survey for gender and for number of employed persons 18 an older per household with any employed person 18 or older. The average design effect for the weighted sample is estimated to be 1.1.

Of the total sample interviewed, 2,877 were wage and salaried workers.

1992 National Study of The Changing Workforce

The 1992 NSCW survey[13] was conducted by Mathematica Policy Research using a questionnaire developed by the Families and Work Institute. Hour-long telephone interviews were completed with a national cross-sectional sample of 3,381 employed men and women ages 18 through 64, as well as 337 women who had dependent children and who were not in the labor force by their own choice—for a total of 3,718. Data were collected from late March through September 1992. Cash incentives ranging from $10 to $15 were offered, and up to 10 phone calls were made to determine household eligibility. Interviewers coded all open-ended responses.

The sampling design and methodology parallels that of the 1997 survey, with the following exceptions: 1) Workers 65 or more years old were not eligible for inclusion, and 2) workers 18 through 24, minority workers, and women not in the labor force were oversampled.

Among 4,493 eligible households, 3,718 interviews were completed—*a completion rate of 83 percent.* Dividing the number of completed interviews (3,718, including nonemployed women with children) by the number of households of known eligibility (4,493) plus the estimated number of eligible households among those where eligibility could not be determined (.634*4,537) yields an *overall response rate of 50.5 percent for potentially eligible households.*

Because of deliberate oversampling of Hispanics, African Americans, nonemployed women, and young workers, it was necessary to adjust the proportions for these groups in the sample by weighting. A two-step procedure was employed in constructing weights. First, households in the sample were iteratively weighted to match their estimated distribution in

---

13. Galinsky, E., Bond, J.T., and Friedman, D.E. (1993). *The Changing Workforce: Highlights of the National Study.* New York: Families and Work Institute.

the population. Second, individual cases were weighted to account for differing probabilities of selection within households. A third step was added for the wage and salaried subsample used for analyses in the 1993 report and here. After comparing select demographic characteristics of wage and salaried workers with characteristics of wage and salaried workers in the March 1992 Current Population Survey (CPS), individual cases were weighted to bring the sex ratio for the sample in line with CPS estimates. The average design effect for the weighted wage and salaried sample was estimated to be 1.22.

Of the total sample, 2,958 were wage and salaried workers.

1977 Quality of Employment Survey

The Survey Research Center of the Institute for Social Research at the University of Michigan was responsible for all data collection. For the cross-sectional sample, a multistage-area probability design was used to select 2,850 households in 74 different geographic areas of the contiguous 48 states.[14] A total of 1,515 face-to-face interviews were conducted in respondents' homes in the fall of 1977.

Sample eligibility was limited to one person per household who 1) worked for pay or other monetary gain at least 20 hours per week, 2) was 16 or more years old, and 3) could be interviewed in English.

Of the 2,850 households in the sample, 733 were determined to be ineligible and 1,926 eligible[15]. Of 1,926 persons selected from eligible households, 1,515 granted interviews—*a completion rate of 79 percent*. Eligibility could not be determined for the remaining 191 households. Dividing the number of completed interviews (1,515) by the number of known eligibles (1,926) plus the number of estimated eligibles among households where eligibility could not be determined (.724*191) yields an *overall response rate of 73.4 percent for potentially eligible households*.

Weighting of the sample was limited to weighting individuals by the number of eligibles in their households. The average design effect for the weighted sample is estimated to be 1.2.

Of the total sample interviewed, 1,311 were wage and salaried workers.

---

14. Quinn, R.P., and Staines, G.L. (1979). *The 1977 Quality of Employment Survey.* Ann Arbor, MI: Institute for Social Research, University of Michigan.

15. The numbers provided by Quinn and Staines (1977) for households of known eligibility, known ineligibility, and unknown eligibility vary slightly across pages 5, 20, and 21. We have selected the most repeated number of eligible households (selected respondents)—1,926—and the once mentioned number of households of known ineligibility—733—to estimate the number of households of unknown eligibility [2850-(1926+733)=191].

A Note on Response Rates

When estimating response rates (above), we follow the conservative guidelines of the Council of American Survey Research Organizations (CASRO). The procedures often used for calculating response rates in market research surveys, for example, produce much higher estimates of response. Applying the algorithm used by one organization to the 1997 NSCW survey, for example, yields a response rate of 62.6 percent, 10 percentage points higher that the rate we report.

No wonder many survey research firms have turned to less rigorous methods for estimating response rates. It is increasingly difficult even to reach people at the other end of a telephone line, not to mention the difficulty of engaging them in conversation with a stranger immediately suspected of wanting to sell them something. In 1997, after much effort, interviewers managed to complete 95 percent of interviews for households where eligibility could be determined. However, it was only possible to determine eligibility for 44 percent of what were thought to be residential telephone numbers. This situation does not bode well for researchers who rely upon telephone interviews to conduct scientifically rigorous survey research.

Data Analysis

All means and percentages are presented for weighted samples, with individual weights having been adjusted by a constant proportion to reproduce actual sample sizes. While cross-sectional tests of differences between means and distributions are also performed on weighted data, regression analyses are performed on unweighted data.

Tests comparing data from different cross-sectional surveys incorporate weighted means or proportions, actual sample sizes or cells counts, and the appropriate design effects for each survey. The Mantel-Haenszel test for linear association is used when evaluating cross-tabulations of ordinal scale variables.

Given the large sizes of most groups compared in this report and the very large number of tests performed, the threshold for reporting differences or relationships as statistically significant was set at $p < .01$.

Sampling Errors

The maximum sampling errors for the total weighted samples in 1997 and 1992 are ± 2 percent at a 95 percent confidence level, while in 1977, it is ± 3 percent.